How to Make
AWARD-WINNING
Teddies

by Michela Rae & Janet Viveiros

Published by Hobby House Press, Inc.
Grantsville, Maryland
www.hobbyhouse.com

Hobby
House
Press
™

Acknowledgements

We would like to take this opportunity to say a personal thank you to all the wonderful bear artists that contributed their work for this book. It is clear that there is so much talent out there and we are grateful that these artists have shared theirs as well as their knowledge with us. There is a myriad of creativity between these pages and we hope it will inspire you, the bear maker, to great new heights.

All the bear portraits were photographed by Raoul Coscia. Lauriel Shelley was responsible for the styling and set designs.

Copyright of Patterns
The patterns in this book are for your personal use and enjoyment. Bears made from these patterns may not be sold.

Additional copies of this book may be purchased at $22.95 (plus postage and handling) from
Hobby House Press, Inc.
1 Corporate Drive, Grantsville, MD 21536
1-800-554-1447
www.hobbyhouse.com
or from your favorite bookstore or dealer.

©2003 by Michela Rae and Janet Viveiros
Second Printing—May 2003

Printed in the United States of America

ISBN: 0-87588-648-5

Table of Contents

Introduction

Welcome to the wonderful world of teddy bears. In this book you will find patterns to make 25 unique bears from award-winning bear artists.

Teddy bears must undoubtedly be the world's favorite collectible animal. They bring us joy and comfort no matter what our age and teddies are truly timeless. A well made bear will last a lifetime and can be passed down through generations if he has been well cared for. A true heirloom! This book is all about making beautiful heirlooms, strong in construction and built to last for years of enjoyment.

Over the years, the art of hand-made teddy bears has developed from seeing teddies sold as a home craft to being sold as a sculpture—a work of art. There are of course various qualities of hand-made bears available; these will vary dramatically in price according to the quality of workmanship, the materials used and more importantly, the artist that made the bear. People will pay more for a beautifully constructed bear that has been well sewn and will keep its shape because it was constructed properly.

This book was written for bear makers who wish to improve and hone their skills to award-winning levels. Each of the 25 artists featured in this book have provided a pattern accompanied by a list of material requirements, special instructions, and hints or recommendations from the artist herself to make your bear making experience as informative and rewarding as possible.

Before you begin making the bears, please read the entire general instructions section. Then sit back, relax and enjoy the bears. Remember this is an opportunity to let yourself go and get those creative juices flowing. Don't be afraid to change the template sizes and have some fun with different colours and textures to create your own unique look.

The patterns and instructions in this book are for making collectible bears for adults. If you wish to make a child's bear, then it is advisable to check the safety standards of children's toys unique to your country and abide by those regulations. This will more than likely involve substituting wooden joints for plastic doll joints and glass eyes for plastic safety eyes.

Should you have any queries about a particular bear, you will find the contact details for each artist at the end of the book. They are there to answer any questions you might have. Please feel free to contact the artists if you need any help.

All of the patterns are shown at actual size unless otherwise stated. For the larger bears, an indication of the enlargement size accompanies the pattern.

Tools of the Trade

This section will give you a basic overview of the materials and equipment required for successful bear making. This is where it all begins. Before you begin, there are a few things you should know.

Fabrics for Bear Making

Great advances in the textile and weaving industries have brought about a very wide range of plush fabrics from which to choose. The colours, textures and styles available are too numerous to mention. We have only covered the most popular fabrics in this section.

Natural Fabrics

Mohair has always been the "fur of choice" amongst most bear makers since the beginning. Sure it's the most expensive option, but it is undoubtedly the most luxurious and most durable. It is available in all sorts of textures, densities, lengths and colors.

The fur lengths vary substantially and it would be wise to select the correct pile length for the size of the bear you wish to make. As an example, a 1-inch pile on a small bear will make it look like an orangutan. Furthermore, the reverse would be a short pile on a large bear, which tends to make it look bald. There is no hard and steadfast rule in bear making. At the end of the day, it depends what look you are after, but it is worthwhile choosing the appropriate length that is in scale with your bear's proportions.

The most common texture finishes available in mohair are sparse, feathered, tufted, matted, swirly, straight, distressed, wavy and string. The terms do tend to vary in different countries.

Another natural fiber, which is also very luxurious, is Alpaca. This fiber comes from an animal related to the Llama. It is very dense and slightly coarser than mohair, but it makes an exquisite fluffy bear and works really well with Polar and Panda bears.

Cotton is also a great alternative. When it is woven into a cotton backing, it makes an excellent bear. Various textures and colors are available.

Synthetic Fabrics

After World War II, toy manufacturers had to look for other alternatives for plush toys due to the shortage and high cost of mohair. This is largely when synthetic fabrics appeared as coats for plush animals. They were cheaper and easier to clean.

There are two types of synthetics available— a knit-back fabric and a woven-back fabric. The knit-back fabrics tend to be cheaper, but their backing

fabric stretches, so it would be wise to line the fabric before using it because it generally loses shape when stuffing. Simply iron on some interfacing to control the stretch and then make your bear as usual. A bear made in this fabric also tends to be larger than its mohair counterpart when finished.

The woven-backs are made in a fashion as mohair with a cotton backing and some of them are just as beautiful and luxurious. If you prefer to use a synthetic fabric, this type will produce the best results.

Upholstery Velvet

This fabric seems to be the first choice among mini-bear artists. It is available in a wide range of colors and textures including a long pile that looks like fur, shiny fabric with sparkles and even patterned fabrics with dots or leopard spots. The choice these days seems to be endless for the mini-bear maker. According to many artists, a longer pile is preferable to use because it hides the stitches very well and looks very similar to mohair.

Ultra Suede

An ideal fabric for paw pads, Ultra Suede can also be used to make a small bear. It is available in different thicknesses for different applications. The thinnest of these is ideally suited for mini-bear paw pads and can also be used to make clothing and accessories. It is very flexible and also hides stitches well.

Mini-Mohair

Mohair is also available for mini-bears. It is generally very short with a straight pile. The choice of color and texture is somewhat limited with straight being the most common followed by "felted" mohair. A good consolation is that you can dye the mohair to your choice of color if nothing appeals to you. Fortunately, with the ever-growing demand from mini bear artists, we may see some new innovations in the future.

Paw Pad Fabrics

There is such a wide choice of paw pad fabrics to choose from that it becomes almost as much fun as choosing the fur itself. The fun part about this is that you will need to decide if you want your pads to contrast or match the color of your bear's fur.

If you prefer matching the fur fabric, then the easiest option is to use the reverse side of the mohair as paw pads. Alternatively, choose a color that matches the tone of the fur. It doesn't have to be the same. As long as the shade is similar, it will look great.

If a contrast is what you prefer, then there are no rules. You can try a dark color fabric for light fur, or why not try a completely different color all together. You decide.

The most popular fabric choices for paw pads are Ultra Suede, upholstery velvet, leather, leatherette, genuine suede and of course, the reverse side of mohair.

Bear Fillings

There are many ways to stuff a bear. Here we'll look at the more popular methods.

Polyester Filling (5)

This is a synthetic polyester fiber filling that is very easy to work with and keeps its shape really well. Polyester filling creates a beautiful finish whether you choose to stuff your bear softly or firmly. Work with it by taking small handfuls and maneuvering it into small spaces with your fingers or a specialized stuffing tool.

Excelsior or Wood Wool (4)

This is the traditional filling for bears and stuffed animals and is comprised of long thin wood shavings. The most popular way of using it is to moisten the material to make it more pliable and then to stuff it carefully into the limbs and body. Many artists still prefer this method when making traditional style reproduction bears.

Metal Shot (2)

Metal pellets are used to add that extra bit of weight to your bear. Everyone has a personal preference—some like heavy bears and some prefer bears with no added weight. If you choose to use a metal filling, you will find different sizes and different types of metal available. The most common are lead, steel and copper. Although lead is the heaviest, try not to use it because of its toxicity. To prevent the pellets from moving around, it is advisable to put them into a bag made from calico or an old pair of nylon pantyhose.

Plastic Pellets (3)

These are used to create a squishy beanbag effect, especially in the tummy. It creates a very huggable bear and also affects the way the bear sits or slouches. It can also be used in the limbs to make them feel more substantial. The most popular method of stuffing the limbs is to stuff the hands or feet first. Then add the pellets to the middle of the limb and then secure them with more polyester filling. There is, however, no rule. You can also use it in the hands and feet like many toy manufacturers currently do and then finish by stuffing softly.

Glass Pellets (1)

Glass pellets are used much the same way as the plastic version. They are available in various sizes and can be used in mini bears and their larger counterparts.

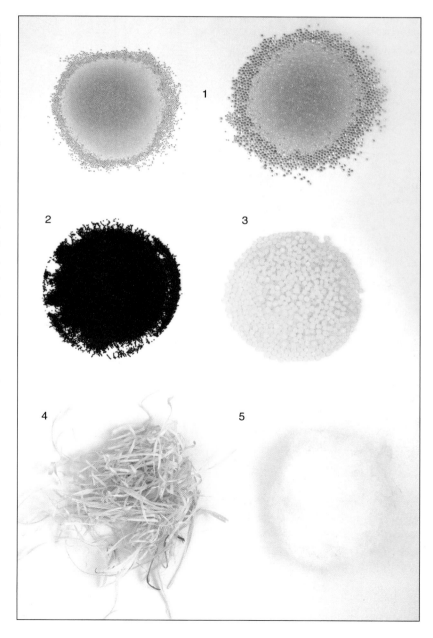

Pattern or Template Making Tools

Your pattern pieces should be made properly if you want to get a lot of use out of them. Remember to always mark your pattern pieces clearly and store different patterns separately for easy reference. There are many substrates available to use as templates with the most common being cardboard.

Cardboard

Cardboard is the easiest material to use for templates because it is so readily available from products you use in your own home or at a store. You would generally use it by photo copying the pattern, pasting the pieces onto the cardboard and then cutting these out to use as templates. The only real disadvantage of cardboard is that with frequent use, it frays or softens around the edges and could end up distorting the finished pieces of your bear, especially the smaller ones.

Acetate

Acetate is a clear stiff plastic material available at your stationery store. You could also use old X-ray film or overhead transparency film. This material is by far the most durable to use as templates and it won't lose its shape. Simply place the acetate over the pattern, trace the pieces and then cut your templates.

General Bear Construction Tools

Scissors

1. Paper scissors are ideal for cutting out your paper or acetate pattern pieces.
2. Use small sharp fabric scissors for cutting your material pattern pieces. Remember always to cut only the backing and not the fur.
3. A pair of very small sharp scissors is ideal for trimming facial fur.

Hemostats

4. and 5. Available in various sizes, hemostats are used for turning body pieces out after they have been sewn. They are mostly used for smaller bears.

Eyes

6. Glass eyes come in a variety of colors and sizes to suit your requirements. The eyes shown here are more commonly available and include solid black glass, colored glass with black pupils, antique shoe buttons and hand-painted eyes for a more realistic effect.

7. Test eyes are a great way to determine the eye size most suitable for your bear. These are available for small, medium and large bears and will save you a lot of valuable time.

Fray Prevention

8. Some woven fabrics tend to fray quite easily and become frustrating to work with. Using a fray prevention liquid around your pattern piece edges before you cut them out will make your bear-making experience far more pleasurable.

Nose Templates

9. These are ready-made self-adhesive felt templates available at most bear supply stockists in various shapes and sizes. Simply stick them on and embroider over the template with a satin stitch.

Sounds

10. and 11. Music boxes, growlers and squeakers can add an extra dimension to your bear. Follow the manufacturer's instructions for insertion. A handy hint when inserting a growler is to enclose it a bag made from muslin or pantyhose. This prevents dust from settling on the mechanism.

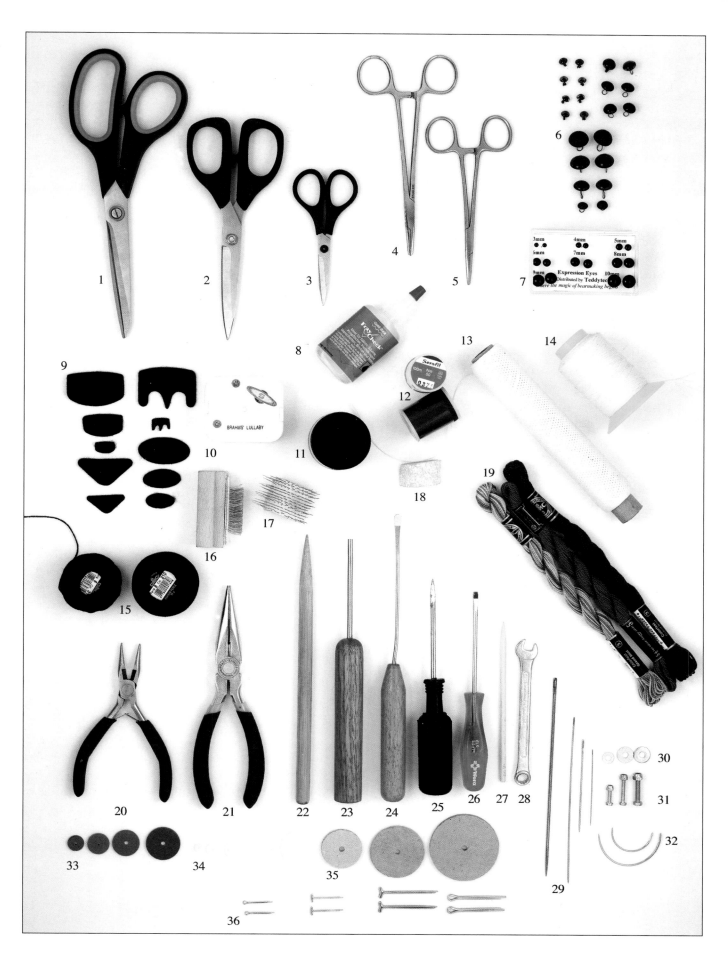

Threads

12. Use a strong multi-purpose thread for machine sewing. There is such a vast array of colors available to choose from making it possible to match your bear's fabric almost exactly. It is very important to use a thread that matches your bear's fur so that when the bear is firmly stuffed, the seam stitches will blend in.

13. Bear maker's floss, dental floss or artificial sinew are absolute necessities in bear making. This is a very strong substance available in different thicknesses. It is used predominantly for inserting eyes and doing needle sculpture, but the thinner thread is also suitable for closing seams. The waxed thread prevents it from slipping and is therefore much easier to use when securing eyes.

14. Hand sewing thread is generally thicker and stronger than machine-sewing varieties. It is used for hand stitching bears and also for tacking/over sewing pattern pieces. Using a thread like this for tacking will make your seams much stronger and more durable. It is highly recommended.

15. and 19. Embroidery threads for noses and claws are available in assorted colors and strand thickness. Perle cotton appears to be the choice of most bear makers. Use a thinner strand for small bears and a thicker one for big bears. Rainbow yarns are also gaining popularity for creating interesting colored noses.

Brushes

16. and 17. Teasel brushes are an important part of bear making. They are used to brush away hair that has been trapped in seams after the pieces have been turned out. Brushing the seams of your bear properly will go a long way towards the neatness of its final appearance.

Waxes

18. Some bear makers like to use bee's wax to polish their bear's finished nose. This is achieved by rubbing the wax over the nose in a brisk upward or downward movement and then buffing the wax with brown paper. This creates a beautiful hard and shiny little nose. Other methods are also used to great effect like epoxy resin or varnish painted on the nose after the embroidery is completed. When using these methods it is imperative to mask the fabric around the nose to protect it if a spill occurs. Use ordinary masking tape for this procedure and remove it when your nose is complete.

Bee's wax can also be used to strengthen your sewing thread. By coating your thread lightly with the wax, you will find it becomes stronger and does not slip. To do this, simply run your thread over the surface of the wax a few times until it feels a little tacky and a wax build-up is visible.

Jointing and Stuffing

20. and 21. Needle/Long nose pliers are indispensable for jointing.

23. A cotter pin turner is one of those tools that makes life a bit easier. Use it to turn your pins and then use the pliers to secure them in place.

22; 24; and 27. These are tools used for stuffing. Choose the one that you are most comfortable with bearing in mind that the sharp point can damage the fur if you use it too vigorously.

25. An awl is used gently to make holes for the joints. NEVER use scissors because they will cut the fabric. Use the awl or a skewer stick and gently, in a circular motion, press the awl through the fabric at the joint position. This way you will separate the weave of the fabric without damaging it.

26. and 28. Screw drivers and a socket wrench are used to secure the nut and bolt jointing system.

30. Metal washers are available in different sizes to suit the size of your jointing system. They are used to protect the joint discs from wearing.

31. Nuts and bolts are available in different sizes for small or large bears.

33; 34; and 35. Joint Discs are available in fibre board, plastic and wood. All are durable. Wooden discs are most commonly used but the red fibreboard discs are more popular for miniature bears.

18. Cotter pins and T-pins are both used in the pin jointing system. Both have two pins that are s p l a y e d first and then turned backwards.

Needles and Pins

29. A good assortment of needles is required here. The most commonly used needles are quilting, sharps, or fine embroidery for hand-stitching; long doll needles for attaching eyes; darner needles for embroidering noses and claws.

32. Curved needles are quite useful for attaching ears. Use glass head or quilting pins because they are easier to use when working with furs.

General Bear Making Instructions

(Instructions provided by Eunice Beaton and Dianne Sturgess)

The first thing to do is to photocopy the pattern pieces according to the instructions provided in case an enlargement is required. Then you can do one of two things to make your templates. You can either glue the photocopied pattern onto cardboard and then cut them out or use acetate and trace the pattern, thereafter cutting out the individual pieces, remembering to transfer all important markings like pile direction, joint placements and openings.

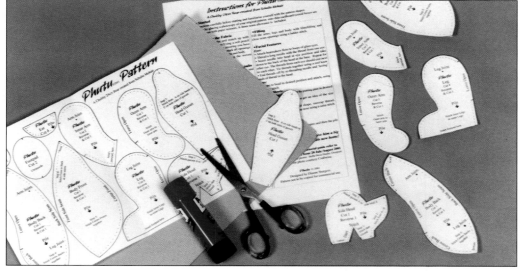

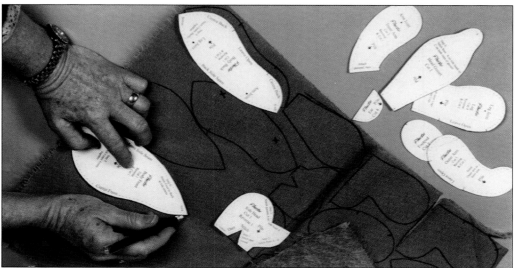

Determine the direction of the fur pile and mark with an arrow on the wrong side of the fabric. Now position your templates on the wrong side of the fabric ensuring the pile direction is matched according to the pattern pieces. Then trace around each piece. Reverse templates where indicated on the pattern to provide a mirror of the shape. Do the same with the paw pads.

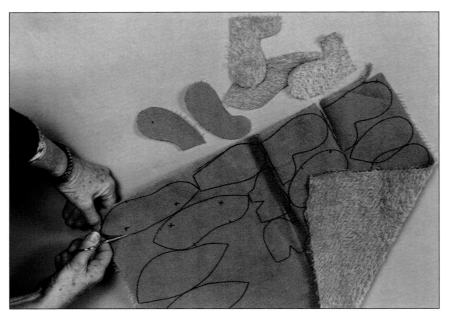

Use small sharp scissors to cut the pieces out. Remember to cut only the backing and not the fur pile. Sew the pieces right sides together with thread that matches the color of the fabric. If you are sewing by hand, a small, firm backstitch is recommended.

For professional results especially on the head of the bear, trim away the fur in the seam allowance on all pieces before you begin pinning them. This provides a smooth finish with no untidy tufts of hair showing through the seams. It is preferable to do this on all pieces, but most importantly the head.

Head and Ears

Pin 2 side head pieces together (right sides inwards) from the nose to the chin. Sew these in place. Then match the center of the nose section on the head gusset to the nose seam on the side head pieces you have just sewn (find this by folding the fabric in half at the nose point and inserting a pin at the middle.) Pin or stitch the gusset in position at this point. Continue to pin from the center outwards until the end of the gusset matches the base of the neck on both of the side head pieces. Leave the bottom open for stuffing and joint

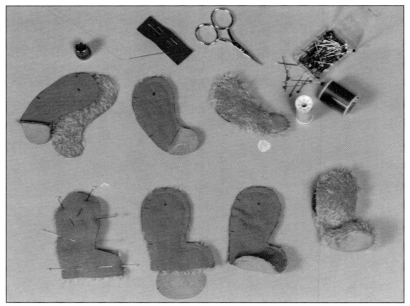

insertion. Tack the head gusset in place with an over sew stitch and then sew by machine or by hand. Turn out the head and brush all trapped fur from the seams.

Pin the ears together in pairs and sew the curved edge leaving the bottom edge open for turning. Turn ears out, brush all hair from seams and then over sew the open edge closed.

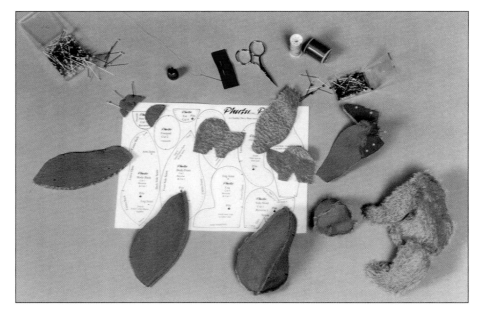

Body

If there are any darts on the body pattern, pin and sew these first. To assemble a two-piece body, pin and sew the body all the way around leaving the opening. Turn out and brush fur from seams. For a four-piece body, pin and sew the two back sections together leaving the opening and then sew the two front sections together at the tummy edge. Attach the front and back sections together at the side seams and sew all the way round. Refer to the pattern pieces to determine whether the neck edge is left open for gathering or not. Turn right sides out and brush fur from seams.

Arms
Two-piece Arm with Paw Pad

Pin and stitch inner arms to paw pads with right sides together. Then attach this to the outer arm and sew leaving an opening where indicated. Turn out and brush fur.

One-piece Arm with Paw Pad
Stitch paw pad to inner arm section with right sides together. Match outer portion with inner arm portion (right sides inwards) and while pressing the paw seam upwards, stitch around the arm leaving the opening where indicated. Turn right sides out.

Legs
One-Piece Leg with Footpad

Fold the leg piece in half on the fold line with right sides facing inwards. Pin and stitch in place leaving the opening where indicated. With legs still wrong side out, place the footpad into the opening at the bottom of the leg by matching the center points of the footpad (fold in half to determine) with the toe and heel position of the leg. Pin and tack in place before sewing all the way round. Clip the seams at the curves and then turn out and brush.

Two-Piece Leg with Footpad

Match the left and right sections of the leg, right sides together. Pin and sew leaving openings where indicated and also the bottom of the leg should be left open to attach the footpad as described above.

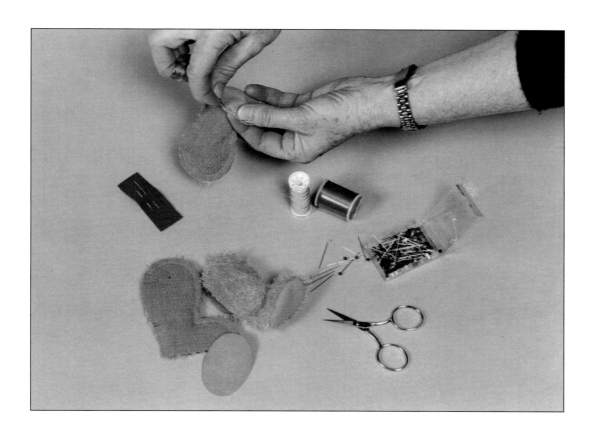

Stuffing the Head

Using the filling of your choice, we recommend polyester fiber, stuff the nose first with small balls of stuffing. Concentrate on achieving the desired look in the muzzle area first and stuff firmly until you are happy with the shape. Look critically at your head to determine that both sides of the head are equally shaped. Remember to leave enough fabric at the bottom for your neck joint.

Now assemble your neck joint in the following order: cotter pin, a metal washer, then the wooden disc. Insert your neck joint into the stuffed head with the pin pointing outwards. Use a strong thread, preferably floss, and sew a gathering or running stitch all the way round leaving about a ¼in or 5mm seam allowance. Start and finish at the back of the neck and pull threads together tightly allowing only the pin to protrude. Knot securely and take loose ends of thread through the head with a needle to further secure placement. Cut ends of thread where they exit and brush head seams.

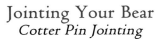

Jointing Your Bear
Cotter Pin Jointing

To assemble the joint, place a cotter pin, a metal washer and a wooden disc together. Make a hole using an awl in the joint positions marked on the inside of the arms, legs and body. To attach the head to the body, make a small hole at the neck position on the body, insert the pin from the head into this hole. When the pin is through, insert a wooden disc and then a metal washer. Separate the pins by using a household knife. Using a pair of needle-nose pliers, bend the ends of the pin outwards first and then inwards so that you are curling the pins. Make sure they are very tight because when the bear is stuffed, the joints tend to loosen. For the other limbs, insert the first part of the joint on the inside of the limb so that only the pin is protruding. Insert this into the matching joint position on the body and assemble as per the head.

Nut and Bolt Jointing

Thread a washer onto the bolt then insert a wooden disc. With super glue or epoxy, secure these in place and allow to dry. Push the bolt through the hole on the inside of the limb and turn out. Only the bolt should protrude from the limb. Now, insert this bolt into the corresponding hole in the body. Make sure that the paws and toes face the correct way. Working through the back opening of the body, insert a wooden disc and then a metal washer over the bolt. Then attach the locknut. Secure in place using a spanner or a bolt turner.

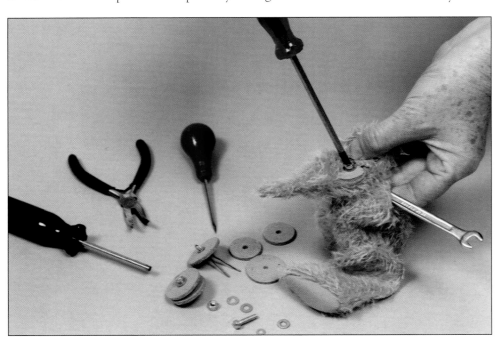

Stuffing the Body and Limbs

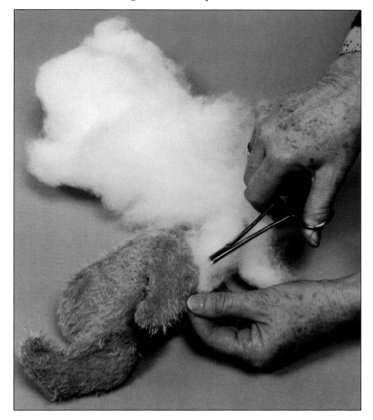

The arms and legs can be stuffed firmly or softly depending on what finish you prefer. The ends of the limbs should be somewhat firmly filled to ensure that the pads are shaped well and that there are no bulges in the seams. If you prefer to use plastic pellets for weight, then stuff the toes and paws first. The pellets should be inserted in the middle of the limb. Complete stuffing till the limb is full ensuring all gaps are filled and then close the open seam with a ladder stitch.

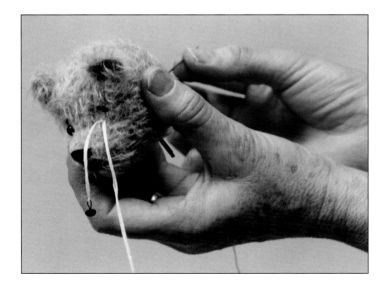

Attaching the Ears

Pin the ears into position until you are happy with their position. Some ears look better when they are slightly curved. Make an anchor stitch at the top, bottom and middle of the ear to hold it in place while you attach it. Use a ladder stitch to attach the ear to the head from the top of the ear to the bottom at the back and then the front. Knot securely and thread loose ends through the head. Cut off the ends. Before you sew the second ear in place, check to see that it is still in line with the first one. If not, make your adjustments now and then sew into position.

Attaching the Eyes

This is a very important feature of your bear because the eyes will create its expression. This part is all about experimentation. Choose the correct eye size by playing around with positioning. Large eyes will make your bear look younger. Smaller eyes will make him look older and perhaps a little quirky. Placement is also very important because of the effects that can be created.

Thread a length of thread through the shank of each eye and loop it. Squeeze the shanks together gently. Trim away the fur from the area where the eyes will be placed. Thread a long doll needle with floss or very strong thread. Waxed floss works well because the wax prevents the thread from slipping out of position. If you have a set of test eyes, use these to find the ideal eye position for your bear. If you don't have these, try using pins with black heads. Hold the head upside down and check that the eyes are evenly spaced from each other and from the tip of the nose. Once you are happy with the placement, make a hole in each position with an awl. Taking the needle, insert it into the first hole and thread it through to come out near the neck joint at either the back of the neck or the bottom of the chin. Leaving one of the threads in the eye position, pull the other one out from the needle so that you now have one thread protruding from the eye and the other from the neck. Now thread the eye onto the needle and then thread the needle through the second eyehole. Insert the second eye and thread the needle through the second hole and out at the neck where your other thread is. Try to get them as close as possible but not in the same hole. Once both of the threads are through, pull the ends to secure the eyes. When you are happy with the outcome, tie a knot. Take the loose threads through the head and cut the ends.

If you would like to create a nose bridge, then you should run the thread between the eye points squeezing them together until sockets are formed.

Nose and Mouth

This is probably one of the most important steps in completing your bear. The way you stitch your nose and mouth will affect the entire expression of the bear. First, decide whether you want a happy, sad, serious or grumpy bear. One of the best ways to experiment with expressions is to use pins and wrap the thread around the various points. Keep changing their position until you are happy with the result. The pinpoints you have chosen will become the entry points for your thread.

Stitch the nose with vertical or horizontal satin stitches remembering to keep an even tension on the stitches so that they aren't too tight or too loose. You can start in the middle working outwards or from left to right. Do what makes you comfortable. Unfortunately, perfect noses come with loads of practice. The good thing is that if you aren't happy with the results, you can unpick the stitches and start again.

This is one area of bear making where you will eventually develop a signature that will identify your bears to collectors. Whether it is in the shape of the nose or the type of mouth you use, you will develop a unique look after a while.

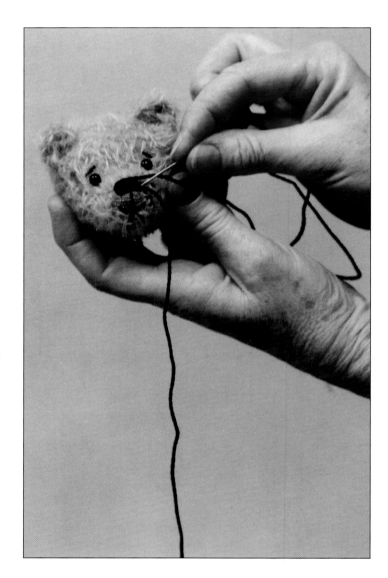

Making Miniature Bears

Basic Tools for Making Miniature Bears

- long darning needle for jointing
- fine sharp needle
- size 10 or smaller needle
- scissors
- hemostats or curved artery forceps
- needle nosed pliers
- hard bristle toothbrush
  Cut the front end of the brush quite short and use it to brush out the fur that gets caught in the seams. After you have finished your bear, a brush with a damp toothbrush picks up the pile of the fur beautifully.
- Fray Check™
- nail clippers
  This is one of those things that you only find out about when your wire cutters go missing and you are in a hurry. Nail clippers are cheap and are perfect for cutting the cotter pins in miniature joints as they can get into such small areas accurately.

General Instructions for Making Miniature Bears

(Instructions provided by Louise Kelly and Megan Wallace)

Stuffing

After sewing, stuffing is the most important part of producing a professional-looking bear. You are basically sculpting the shape of your bear from the inside out, so you must never lose sight of the shape you are trying to create. Keep checking throughout the process that you keep the cheeks equal and the nose section firm. I have my own rather eccentric way of stuffing my bears, which I will share with you, but you may already have your own method. I take a very small amount of polyester stuffing and twist around my hemostats to form a small "cocoon" of hard packed stuffing. Then I slip this off the hemostats and cut it into approximately four small pieces. I stuff my bears very firmly indeed as I find it easier to joint them and embroider the features on a firm background. The body is filled with small glass beads as well as polyester.

General

Paste your pattern templates on a sheet of thin cardboard - cereal boxes work well - and cut out.

Trace the pattern pieces on to the fabric. I like to use Pentel™ milky pens when tracing a pattern onto dark fabric. Cut out on the lines using small sharp scissors.

Head

Sew the two side head pieces together from the neck edge to the nose. Don't cut off your thread when you get to the nose, as you can continue using it to insert the gusset. Sew in the gusset. Turn out and stuff firmly.

Insert joint at neck opening and close securely.

Sew the ears together in pairs leaving the straight edge open. Turn to the right side and sew the straight edge closed. Pin to the head and attach with ladder stitch.

Determine the eye position by sticking glass headed pins into the head. If you wish, you can work a sculpting stitch behind the eyes before inserting them. This will help to shape the head. Insert the eyes and knot off securely at the back of the head. Embroider the nose and mouth with a single strand of black cotton.

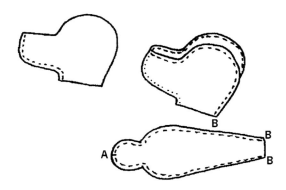

Inserting the Cotter Pin Joint

Using a double length of thread, sew a small running stitch around the neck edge being careful not to pick up any stuffing. Insert the joint. Gently pull the thread until the neck edges fit firmly around the pin. Fasten off and cut the thread.

Positioning the Eyes

1. Thread the beads onto thin pins (lace pins.) You can then pin the eyes in a position that pleases you. Generally this is just above and on the inside of the center head/muzzle seam.

2. Make a small mark where the pins enter the fabric. Thread your needle with a double strand of black thread (I thread the needle with both ends of the thread leaving a loop at the bottom, which I use to secure the thread.) Sew the eyes in place entering at the base of the neck and exiting at the mark you have made on the face. Thread the bead on the needle and return to the base of the neck. Return to the bead and sew through the bead again. Pull gently to sink the bead into the head. Return to the neck. Repeat once more (by this time the bead will be pretty full of thread and you may have to give it a tug to get the needle through.) Fasten off under the head and repeat for the other eye making sure you pull the same amount so that the eyes match.

Ears

Cut two pair of ears from mohair. Clip one pair. Fray Check™ the bottom edge. Sew them together in pairs. Turn right sides out and over sew along the bottom. Bend the ears in half and sew along the bottom again. Position the ears at the top of the head, slightly below the seam line and ladder stitch in place.

Jointing the Head to the Body

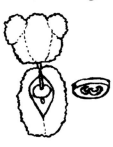

Place the cotter pin from the neck through the hole. Place the other disc inside the body and over the pin. Press the second disc up under the top of the body and bend the two sides of the pin slightly apart. Clip the two sides so that approximately 5/16in-1/2in (.75cm-1cm) remains. Be careful not to cut them too short. Using your long nosed pliers, bend these in so that they coil tightly against the disc inside the body. The head should fit tightly against the body, as it will work slightly looser when you stuff the body.

18

Body

Sew two body pieces together leaving an opening at the back as indicated. Turn out.

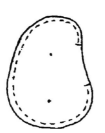

Stuffing the Body

1. Using a small spoon, fill the body as full as you can with the glass beads.

2. Finish filling the body with stuffing, paying great attention to the shoulders and bottom because you will be thread jointing your bear here. I stuff my bears' bodies "like a rock" and they have a lovely heavy feel for such small bears, as well as being easy to joint.

3. Using a double thread, ladder stitch the back closed pulling the threads tight after every few stitches. Always pull the thread downwards as pulling it to the side may rip the fabric. Carefully use your scissors to push in the edges of the fabric and the stuffing as you go. Fasten off neatly and pull the thread through the body. Cut off the thread. If you are using a pin or bolt jointing system, you will stuff the body last.

Arms

One-piece Arm with Paw Pad

1. Cut out the arms reversing the pattern to make a pair. Cut the paw pads out of ultra suede or similar.

2. Sew the paw pads to the arms matching C to C and D to D.

3. Sew around the arms and paw pads from A to B.

4. Turn right sides out by gripping the inside of the paw at the end seam firmly with the hemostats and gently pulling through.

5. Stuff the arms firmly paying special attention to the top of the arm, as you will be jointing here. Ladder stitch the tops closed. You may find it useful to end your thread by finishing it off at the top inside of the arm. This will be against the bear's side and nobody will ever see it. Also, by pulling the thread tight here you will achieve a nice rounded top. This can be done for the legs as well, but you must be careful that you make a left and a right leg if you do so.

Two-piece Arm with Paw Pad

Sew the paw pads to the inner arms. Now put an inner and an outer arm together, right sides on the inside, and sew leaving an opening as indicated. Turn out. Insert cotter pin and disc if you are not going to string joint. Stuff firmly and close opening using ladder stitch. When stuffing a small bear it is always easier to use a hemostat to help place the stuffing in the tips of the hands and toes.

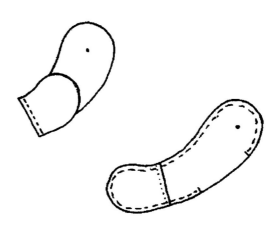

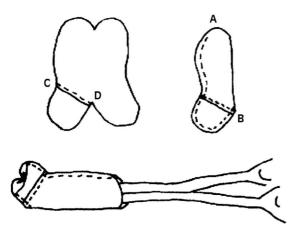

One-Piece Leg

1. Cut out the legs, fold in half and sew from A to B.

2. Cut out the foot pads from ultra suede. Mark the center - front and back. Mark the center back of the leg. Tack the center back of the foot to the center back of the leg. Starting at the center front of the foot, stitch around to the back, undo the tacking stitch and continue to the front. Finish off.

3. Insert the hemostats and grip the toe area firmly. Gently ease the leg through to the right side. Make sure you grip both the ultra suede pad and the mohair with the hemostats, as this will minimize the risk of tearing.

4. Stuff firmly concentrating on the toe and upper leg. Stuff both feet before stuffing the leg as this enables you to match them up more easily.

5. Ladder stitch the top closed.

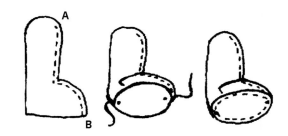

Two-Piece Legs

Match left and right sections of the leg, right sides together. Pin and sew leaving openings where indicated. Attach footpad. Then insert joint if using this system, close seams, and brush.

Thread Jointing

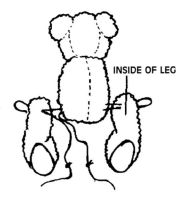

INSIDE OF LEG

1. On such a small bear it is easy to find that the marks have moved enough to give you a very lopsided look, so I find that it is better to push a long pin, approximately 5/16in (.75cm) from the top of each leg and pin it onto the side of the bear, about 5/16in (.75cm) up from the bottom seam. Check that your bear is balanced and mark where the pin has entered at the side of the bear and the inside of each leg.

2. Take a length of bear makers floss and split it in two (this can be quite tricky.)

3. Take the thicker piece and thread it into a long darning needle.

4. Take one leg and pull the floss through the place you have marked on the inside to the outside of the leg. Re-enter the outside of the leg in EXACTLY the same place and pull the floss back to the inside of the leg a few threads away. This is important or you will have a dimple on the outside of the leg when you join the bear. Check that you haven't split the floss by pulling it gently to see that it runs freely. If it doesn't, start again, but be careful as this will weaken the floss.

5. Enter the place you have marked on the side of the bear and pull the floss through to the mark on the other side. Enter the inside mark of the other leg and repeat as for the first leg.

6. Take two pieces of strong string and knot one end of each to the ends of the floss (I do this because the floss is quite expensive and although you need a fairly long piece to pull, most of it is going to be cut off and thrown away.)

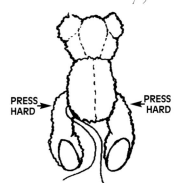

PRESS HARD   PRESS HARD

7. Tie a half-knot — over and under once — between the bear and the leg.

8. Now you need somebody else's help. Get them to grip the bear very tightly at the top of the legs, between their thumb and finger from the front. You need to have the threads facing you from the back. Take the threads and pull them very tightly and, without loosing the tension, complete the half-knot. Knot tightly once more and cut the threads close to the leg. Push the remaining ends gently under the leg with the point of your scissors.

William
2½in (6cm). Fully jointed mini bear with stenciled paw and footpad detail.

The Artist
Antonette Botha–Antonette's Tiny Teddies

I made my first bear five years ago, but he didn't look anything like the bear I was attempting to make, so I gave it up thinking that bear making wasn't for me. However, three years later I rediscovered bear making at a hobby show and decided to try my hand at sewing again. This time I was determined to make more than one. After the first two, I was hooked. I then experimented with different patterns and designs, soon after designing my own and finally selling them. My little bear Meadow Mix won first prize at the 2000 South African Spring Bear fair and Little Santa won 1st place at the 9th Annual South African Bear fair in 2001.

Contact Details

Antonette Botha
Antonette's Tiny Teddies
PO Box 6072
Greenhills 1767
South Africa

Tel: +27 (011) 692-3253
Email: antonetteteddies@worldonline.co.za
Website: www.geocities.com/abothateddies

Materials Needed
5in x 5in (13cm x 13cm) mini mohair or upholstery velvet
2in x 2in (5cm x 5cm) beige ultra suede
2in x 2in (5cm x 5cm) brown ultra suede
2mm onyx beads for eyes
ten 5mm disc joints or strong thread for string jointing
embroidery thread for nose (DMC 3790)
dental floss for attaching eyes
polyester filling/steel shot or small glass beads for stuffing

Special Instructions
Please refer to the general bear making instructions covered in the book.

Paw and Foot Pads
Make a stencil of the paw pad using acetate. Cut out paw prints on the beige pair of suede paw pads. Cut out normal paw pads from the darker ultra suede. Glue the two together so that the lighter suede with the cut out prints is on the top of the pad. Stitch to inner arm and then assemble as usual. Do the same for the footpads.

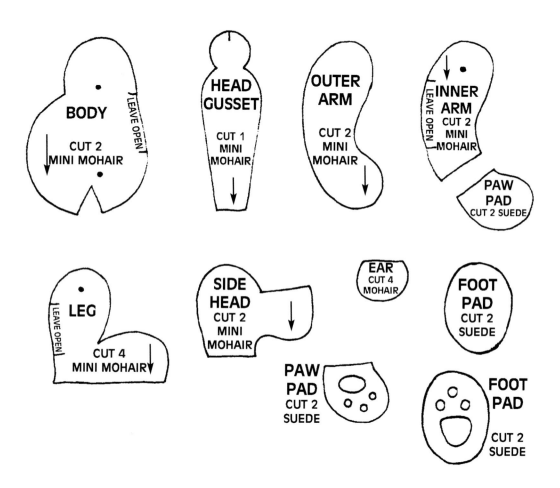

Grizzly Mother and Cub
4in (10cm) long open-mouthed Grizzly bear on all fours with her 2½in (6cm) cub.

The Artist

Cheryl Moss—Mossie Bears

I have been making bears for the past 5 years with miniatures being my favorites. My "biggest" claim to fame is having made the world's smallest fully-jointed, hand-sewn bears. The smallest one is 4.5mm standing and now lives in the new museum in Korea. My bears vary considerably with all of them being one-of-a-kind. They vary from scenes that are all built by hand to groups of teddies. Single bears are usually accessorized in some way. I exhibit regularly at the Hugglets festivals in the UK, as well as in other countries around the world. I still love to see another person's face light up when a bear particularly appeals to them. I have made so many good friends all over the world through the teddies – that is the hobby's greatest income and reward.

Contact Details

Cheryl Moss
Mossie Bears
17 Albrecht Road
Sunward Park, 1459
Gauteng
South Africa

Tel: +27-11-896-4860
Fax: +27-11-896-4860
Email: moss@iafrica.com

Materials Needed

I used a synthetic fabric to create this pair of bears. The reason for this was that it gave them a fairly realistic look for their size having the correct color, pile and texture. This is a personal preference, however, and you may prefer a different appearance achieved by using a short pile mohair or alpaca fabric. Always choose your fabrics carefully. They contribute greatly to the character of your bear.

The materials listed below are sufficient to make both bears.
- 10in x 7in (25cm x 18cm) mini mohair or similar material:
  ($^2/_{16}$-$^3/_{16}$in [3mm-4mm] pile)
- 3½in x 3½in (9cm x 9cm) square matching ultra suede or similar material
- 1in x 1in (3cm x 3cm) pink or red ultra suede for mouth
- two pairs 2mm onyx or glass beads for eyes
- ten 6mm rounded discs
- ten 12mm rounded discs
- ten cotter pins – rounded or T-shape – as thin as possible
- hemostat or tweezers
- polyester filling
- basic teddy bear sewing kit

Optional
- Fray Check™ or Fray Stoppa™
- fabric paint for foot and paw pad detail
- steel or lead shot for extra weight

Special Instructions

This pattern is to make an open-mouthed, 4in (10cm) long Grizzly bear on all fours and her 2½in (6cm) cub.

Please read through all instructions before starting. I have given you a few options every now and then, and you need to choose which ones you are taking before you start cutting out the pattern. If you are a beginner, it is recommended that you make a few basic teddy bears before attempting this slightly more complicated pattern. I also recommend that you attend a local teddy bear class even if you are a more experienced bear maker. A great deal can be learned from sharing ideas and techniques.

Tracing and Cutting Out Pattern

Trace all the pattern pieces as required onto cardboard or stencil plastic and cut them out. Set them out on the mohair and the ultra suede as shown on the pattern layout sheet. Follow the direction of the fur pile as shown on the pattern layout. Make all markings on the back of the fabric – it is recommended that this is done with a pencil or a gel pen so that Fray Check™

or Fray Stoppa™ can be applied to the edges before sewing. Normal ink may mark through the fabric. Allow the fabric to dry before cutting out. When you cut out, cut only through the fabric backing, avoiding the fur pile.

Stitching

A small seam allowance of 1/16in or 2mm is allowed. Should you prefer a larger seam allowance, cut away from the pattern edges as required. All pieces are sewn with the fur inside. Pin the pieces together first and, after sewing, use a stiff brush or a pin to pick the fur out of the seams. The type of stitch used is largely optional, but sew all seams twice. Use matching or invisible thread and keep all stitches as small as possible. Check for any small gaps in the seams before turning.

Turning

As these bears are small, a hemostat or tweezers are necessary to turn the pieces. It is recommended that you grip only the seams when turning and use minimum force or you will tear through the fabric.

Head

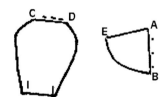 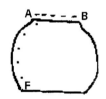

I always prefer to make the head of the bear completely before carrying on so that I can see the character of the bear emerge as I go. This is a personal preference, however, and not a rule.

I have included an inset muzzle in the pattern. Should you wish your bear to have a shaved muzzle, simply draw around the muzzle pieces alongside the side head and muzzle as if they were already joined. Then trim away the areas you would like to shave or pluck them with a pair of tweezers. Do this before you sew so that no fur is trapped in the seams, as it is difficult to remove afterwards. You may also prefer to make the ears out of the same fabric instead of contrasting them as I have done. Please note that the cub's ears are nearly the same size as those of the mother bear. This is done so that they appear proportionately larger.

Begin by sewing the muzzle pieces to the side head from A - B and the nose to the gusset as shown in the diagram from C - D. Then join the two side head pieces together from E - F. If you wish the adult bear

to have an open mouth, you need to insert the mouthpiece just after sewing the two side head pieces together. Cut a straight line through the muzzle from G - H and then attach the inner mouthpiece by fitting it in and sewing all around the open edges (see diagram below.)

Once this is done, attach the head gusset to the side head pieces. Attach it at points A and E and then sew around the areas between the points. Once the nose has been securely sewn, sew around the sides marked E to I. Leave the area between I and F open for stuffing. Turn the head and stuff it firmly, starting from the nose and mouth. Shape the head as you are stuffing to get the desired curves. Be careful if you are trying to create an open mouth effect so that the mouth area is not overstuffed. Take note when the face has started to take on the desired shape. While needle sculpting can do a great deal for a bear, the best time to shape its character is in the stuffing.

Once the head is fully stuffed, it is time to fit the joint on the mother bear (the cub has an all-in-one head and body and does not require a joint.) Push the cotter pin through the disc to make a joint. Place the joint in the opening and then gather the fabric together around it using strong thread. Only the two long pieces of the cotter pin must be sticking out so that the head appears to be on a pin.

Continue sewing down the body pieces of the cub once the head seams are sewn leaving a small opening under the tummy. It is recommended that you do this before you try to stuff the head

Decide on the position of the eyes once the head has been closed. Mark them with a pin or a pen making sure they are evenly placed. Using strong thread, come up through the base of the neck and out where the eye is to be fixed. Thread the eye onto the needle and then go back through the same hole and down to the neck again. Pull the eye in tight so it appears to be a little sunken in. If you are using looped glass eyes, you may have to make a small hole for the loop to go into. Fasten the thread tightly under the neck and then repeat with the other eye.

Sew around the ears as shown. Turn them and close in the base. You may stuff them for a fuller look or leave them flatter. For the bears in this pattern, I gathered in the base of the ear and left it unstuffed. Position the ears on the head with pins and sew them to the head using a ladder stitch around both sides once you have achieved the desired effect. Make sure they are even and firmly fixed to the head.

Embroider the nose and mouth once using a dark thread. If you are unsure about the correct shape of the nose, cut a few examples out of dark material. When you have decided on the best one, glue it on and then embroider over it using even stitches. This should prevent the need for frequent attempts and lots of unpicking.

Body and Legs

 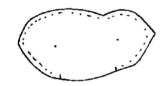

Join the matching sides of the legs together leaving an opening at the back. Then attach the foot pads as shown. Mark the center points on each foot pad before sewing — it helps to keep it in place. Sew the body of the mother bear leaving a small opening under the tummy.

You can use a stitch jointing system if you prefer it to the cotter pins. If you choose to do this, stuff and close the body as well as the legs before running a long piece of strong thread through the legs and the body several times. Be careful that you come out at the same point in the leg every time so that the leg can turn easily and make sure that you tie off the thread very soundly and hide it in the joint. Otherwise, the cotter pin method is explained in the next paragraphs.

Turn all the pieces. Take 8 cotter pins, flatten their heads, (or use T-pins instead) and put them into discs. Put the joints into the legs and push the pins through where the joints are marked. Stuff the legs firmly making sure the ends of the cotter pins cannot be felt through the other sides. Using a ladder stitch, neatly close up all the openings.

Attach the legs to the body with the cotter pins and push the discs onto the cotter pins inside of the body.

Curl the halves of the cotter pins tightly against the disc on each limb. Line up the mother bear's head and push the cotter pin through the neck. Add the disc on the inside of the neck and curl the ends as you have done with the others. It is sometimes a good idea to use a much smaller disc inside the neck as it doesn't push out against the material around the neck as a bigger one sometimes does.

You can stuff the bodies with stuffing and you can add some lead or stainless steel pellets for extra weight. Correctly placed in the bottom, they will make the bears sit a lot more easily. If you are concerned about the safety aspect of lead, make a small cloth bag in which to sew the pellets first. Use a spoon or a tiny funnel to get them into the bears without too much mess.

Finish off the bears by closing up the bodies and brushing out all the seams. If you wish to add any paw pad detail, use a fabric marker and embroider on the claws. You can also use a thin marking pen to mark around the edges of the open mouth.

ATTACH MUZZLE HERE

ADULT SIDE HEAD
CUT 2 (1 REV)

ADULT NOSE
CUT 1

SLIT PLACEMENT FOR OPEN MOUTH

ADULT SIDE MUZZLE
CUT 2 (1 REV)

JOINT

ADULT BACK LEGS
CUT 4 (2 REV)

INNER MOUTH
CUT 1
FROM PINK ULTRA SUEDE

ADULT GUSSET
CUT 1

JOINT

ADULT FRONT LEGS
CUT 4 (2 REV)

ADULT EAR
CUT 4
2 FROM SUEDE

ADULT BODY
CUT 2 (1REV)

LEG JOINT

ARM JOINT

BABY SIDE MUZZLE
CUT 2 (1 REV)

BABY HEAD GUSSET
CUT 1

BABY FOOT PAD
CUT 4

BABY BACK LEG
CUT 4 (2 REV)

BABY FRONT LEG
CUT 4 (2 REV)

BABY NOSE
CUT 1

BABY EAR
CUT 4 2 FROM SUEDE

BABY BODY
CUT 2 (1 REV)

BABY SIDE HEAD
CUT 2 (1 REV)

ADULT FOOT PAD
CUT 4

Clooney
3½in (9cm). Bear fully-jointed with shaded face detail.

The Artist
Megan Chamberlain–Megan of Essential Bears

Her love of bear making began in 1992 when she decided to challenge herself by making a really tiny bear. Little did she know that that scaled down pattern would result in what has now become her profession. Her impeccably crafted creatures with her hallmark, personal style are highly sought after and extremely collectible. Exclusive teddy bear shops in the UK, USA, Germany and Switzerland commission her to make bears for their customers. She also has a very dedicated following of collectors who visit her table year after year at international bear fairs. In fact, many of her bears are sold via the internet before she has even left South Africa en route to an overseas destination.

The innumerable awards she has won endorse Megan's sparkling international reputation. She was honored with winning places in the Teddy Bear Club International Magazine Miniature Bear of the Year Professional Category (2000) as well as in the Linda Mullin's San Diego Fair (2002) and has been nominated for the prestigious TTTA 2002 Award in Japan. She has also won many accolades in her own country, a highlight being named "The Bear Person of the Year 2001" at the Buitenverwachting Bear Fair. Her art has been featured in many publications including the *Australian Bear Creations, Wonderful World of Teddy Bears, Teddy Bear Club International, Teddy Bear Scene, Teddy Bear Review* and *Teddy Bear & Friends*.

"We live in the beautiful city of Cape Town, South Africa. Our studio is situated in an old Cape cottage-style house with a wonderful view of the mountains. This is also the home of the Cape Teddy Bear Supply Company where we hold regular workshops and have a selection of patterns, kits and an extensive range of bear makings."

Contact Details

Megan Chamberlain
Essential Bears
18 Long Street
Mowbray, Cape Town
South Africa

Tel: +27-21-685-3487
Email: ebears@iafrica.com
Website:
http://users.iafrica.com/e/eb/ebears

Materials Needed
10½in (27cm) square of upholstery fabric
matching ultra suede for paw pads
two 6mm joints and one cotter pin
two 2mm onyx beads for eyes
black embroidery thread for nose
extra strong thread for jointing
polyester filling

Special Instructions
NB
A seam allowance of ⅛in or 3mm is included in the pattern. Please refer to the miniature bear making instructions covered at the front of the book.

Finishing

Stuff the head using small quantities of stuffing ensuring that the nose is well shaped. Make sculpted eye sockets before inserting the eyes. Mark the position of the eyes with pins. Using strong thread, insert the needle through the neck opening bringing the needle out in the first eye position. Leave sufficient thread at the back of the neck to tie threads off. Take a small stitch; then take thread across to other eye position. Once again, take a small stitch emerging at the back of the neck. Tie the threads together securely using your fingers to "sculpt" the eye sockets. Insert the jointing disc and cotter pin into the base of the head. Using two strands of very strong thread or dental floss, gather the base of the head tightly over the disc. Cut the thread. Knot the two pieces of thread together tightly then thread each piece singly and bury in the head. Insert bead eyes using beading needle and fine thread. Embroider the nose and mouth. Stitch the ears to the head using ladder stitching shaping into a rounded curve.

Thread Jointing

With this type of jointing, it is important to remember that threads must move freely at all times. Do not stitch through the thread. Use a fine line pen to mark the position on body for arms and legs remembering to mark inside arms and legs as well. Using a long needle and strong thread used double, insert needle through body at leg placement leaving long ends hanging free. Insert needle into leg slightly to the side of the pen mark exiting on other side of mark. A small stitch has been taken through the fabric and stuffing. Go back into the body just slightly away from previous stitch and exiting on other side. Repeat the process attaching the other leg to the body. Exit near the first stitch. Remove needle and knot all ends together securely, pulling legs against body. Thread ends on needle and bury in body stuffing. Repeat for arms.

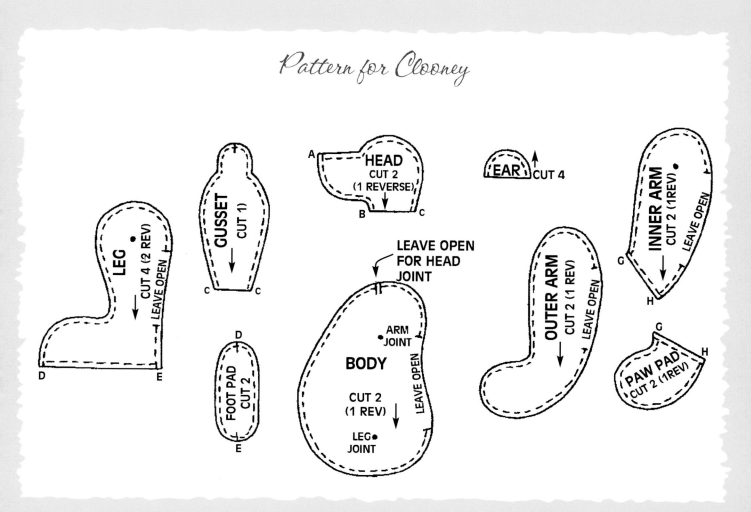

Pattern for Clooney

Mr. Potts

4in (10cm). Character bear with robe, hat and glasses.

The Artist

Megan Wallace—Tin Soldiers

My bear making mania started in an innocent way many years ago when I wanted to make a teddy for my little sister who is a soft toy freak. At the time, I could not find a teddy bear pattern at our local library, or in a sewing shop, and no one seemed to be able to suggest suitable materials to use if you did not want to work with synthetic plush. I "designed" the pattern for my first bear by looking at the way a store-bought bear was constructed and used corduroy dress fabric. The bear was an instant hit, and I continued making similar bears, just a little smaller each time. A miniature bear artist was born!

A few years later, when real teddy bear-making materials finally became available in South Africa, my bear making career really took off. I was inundated with orders for small bears from my friends, and everyone wanted to learn how to make them too. I have been running the Tin Soldiers Studio for several years now, teaching beginners and advanced bear making techniques. We sell all manners of bear making supplies, specializing in miniature bears. I also teach at least two classes a week and simply can't keep up with the demand.

I have designed several patterns that are available commercially on my website and I am adding to the collection slowly. In the recent past I have had the honor to be invited to design a limited edition bear for the Melrose House Museum. The bear turned out to be so popular that I have been asked to design another one to add to the collection every year for the last three years. These bears all have bearing on the history of the museum and are becoming famous in their own right. I have also designed a set of bears that were used by the South African Mint on a coin set for babies, and at the moment, I am working on special commission to a South African celebrity.

For me, the pleasure of bear making still lies in creatively bringing together the right materials and design and patiently crafting a truly stunning critter.

Contact Details

Megan Wallace
Tin Soldier Studio
278 Hiperbool Street
Meyerspark, 0184
South Africa

Tel: +27-12-803-8095
Mobile: +27-83-305-5954
Email: soldier@lantic.net
Website: www.tinsoldiers.co.za

Materials Needed

½ square non-shiny mini velvet in teddy bear color for head and limbs
1 square shiny mini velvet or glitter mini velvet in a dark color for body and coat
one set 5mm mini bear joints
one pair 2mm onyx beads
black embroidery thread for nose and claws
small scrap of ultra suede for footpads
matching threads for fabric and general sewing supplies.
Accessories:
   pair of miniature glasses and a wand
   gold glitter glue
   small gold sequins or glitter stars and gold beads for buttons

Special Instructions

Miniature bears are made the same way as bigger bears. Sew by hand using a small tight running stitch and keep your seams very narrow. When I made my wizard, I cotter pin jointed the head, and used string jointing for the arms and legs. If you wish, you may cotter pin joint the arms and legs as well. If this is your first miniature bear, good luck, and remember that patience and working carefully will result in a bear good enough to take pride of place in your collection.

General

Tip: I like to use Pentel™ milky pens when tracing a pattern onto dark fabric. Cut out on the lines using small sharp scissors avoiding cutting the pile and only cutting the fabric backing.

Legs

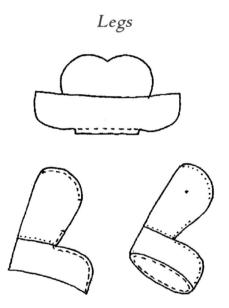

Sew the leg pieces to the feet. Then fold each leg in half and sew the seams leaving an opening where indicated. Insert footpad. Turn right side out and stuff firmly (remember cotter pin joint if you are not thread jointing.) Close opening with a ladder stitch. Tip: if you would like the bear to stand on its own, put glass beads or a small quantity of lead shot into the feet when stuffing.

Arms

Because there are sleeves, paw pads are for both sides of the arm. Attach pads to corresponding arms, match pairs and sew in place leaving openings where indicated.

Jointing

Push the head cotter pin into the body at marked joint position; slip over the second disc and turn the cotter pin ends. If you are cotter pin jointing the rest of the bear, repeat for arms and legs. If you are string jointing, stuff the body and close the opening with a ladder stitch before attaching the arms and legs.

Hat

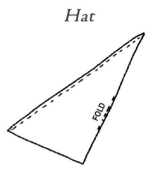

Fold hat in half on fold line and sew up the long end. Turn right side out and stuff lightly. The hat is attached to the head with ladder stitch.

Coat

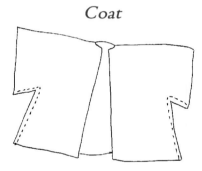

Sew up the under arm seams and turn right side out. Decorate with glitter and sequins if desired. Tip: it's a good idea not to put your stars and sequins too close to the edge of the coat, and stay away from fold areas i.e. the underarm.

Finishing Touches

Mr. Potts has 4 claws on each hand and on his feet. This is optional. I felt that the black claws balanced the contrast in color between the bear and its outfit.

Use small gold beads to put buttons on the bear's body if desired.

The magic wand is made from a toothpick that is cut to a length of 3cm. Paint it black with a golden tip.

The glasses are made from thin brass wire. You will need round-nose pliers and a bit of skill to make these. Ready-made glasses for miniature bears are available from teddy bear stockists.

Pattern templates for Mr. Potts

(Cut these from black or glitter velvet)

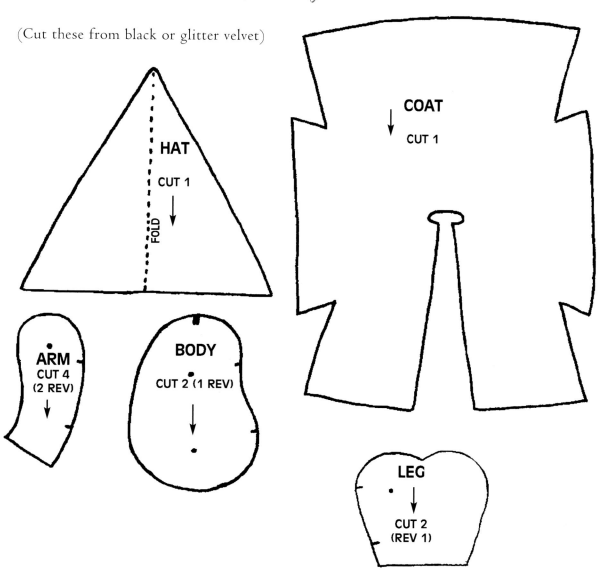

HAT
CUT 1
FOLD

COAT
CUT 1

ARM
CUT 4
(2 REV)

BODY
CUT 2 (1 REV)

LEG
CUT 2
(REV 1)

(Cut these from teddy bear color mini velvet)

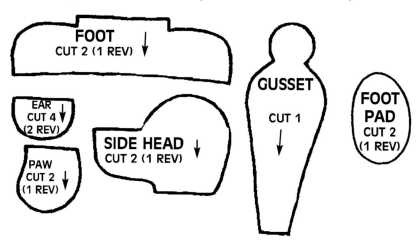

FOOT
CUT 2 (1 REV)

EAR
CUT 4
(2 REV)

PAW
CUT 2
(1 REV)

SIDE HEAD
CUT 2 (1 REV)

GUSSET
CUT 1

FOOT PAD
CUT 2
(1 REV)

Ming-Yi
3¼in (8cm). Panda bear fully-jointed with wobble head joint and shaded face detail.

The Artist
Wendy Chamberlain–Wendy of Essential Bears

Wendy's bear making began in a humble way over ten years ago when she was encouraged by her daughter, Megan, to make a bear featured in a soft toy book on loan from the local library. Megan's delight at the ensuing ursine creature inspired her to make another, and yet another – all the while perfecting, by honest practice, the skill of creating that elusive quality "character." Since 1994, this hard work has been rewarded by a solid international reputation and a growing following of serious, dedicated collectors who are happy to wait for months on waiting lists for very exclusive, limited edition bears. Perhaps that is what inspires Wendy most – the obvious enjoyment she brings to so many people through the magnificent workmanship of her creatures. Wendy's skill and imagination has won accolades worldwide including first place in the prestigious Linda Mullins San Diego Bear Fair in 2002 and numerous South African awards, a highlight being named "Teddy Bear Artist of the Year" at the Stellenbosch Teddy Bear Fair in 2001. She has been nominated for the TITA 2002 Award in Japan.

Her work is on permanent display/exhibit in museums in the USA, Switzerland and Korea. She is regularly featured in publications such as *Teddy Bear Friends*, *Teddy Bear Review*, *Teddy Bear Club International*, *Wonderful World of Teddy Bears* and *Teddy Bear Scene*. These achievements are never taken for granted by Wendy who is always enchantingly excited by the respect, acclaim and recognition she wins for her artistry.

Contact Details

Wendy Chamberlain
Essential Bears
18 Long Street
Mowbray, Cape Town
South Africa

Tel: +27-21-685-3487
Email: ebears@iafrica.com
Website:
http://users.iafrica.com/e/eb/ebears

Materials Needed
small pieces of upholstery velvet in brown and cream
matching ultra suede for paw pads
two 9mm joints and one cotter pin
two 2mm onyx beads for eyes
embroidery thread for nose
extra strong thread for jointing
polyester filling
fabric pen for eye socket detailing
silk ribbon roses and small piece of green silk ribbon (optional)

Special Instructions
NB
Seam allowance of $1/8$ in or 3 mm included in pattern.

Body
First stitch the top and bottom body pieces together. Then stitch around entire body piece leaving a small hole on the top of the body for the cotter pin to be inserted and leaving an opening in the back for stuffing.

Finishing

Stuff the head using small quantities of stuffing and ensuring that the nose is well shaped. Insert the jointing disc and cotter pin into the base of the head. Using two strands of very strong thread or dental floss, gather the base of the head tightly over the disc. Cut the thread and knot the two pieces of thread together tightly. Then thread each piece singly and bury in the head. Using the fabric pen, "paint" eye detailing on face before inserting eyes. Allow to dry well. Then using beading needle and fine thread, insert eyes.

Embroider the nose and mouth. Stitch the ears to the head using a ladder stitch shaping into a rounded curve. Push the cotter pin through the hole at the top of the body. Place second disc on the pin and turn ends over tightly. The head should be firmly on the body. Stuff the body carefully ensuring that the stuffing is even. Close up the back opening. Stuff arms and legs firmly and close back seams using a ladder stitch. Stitch silk ribbon roses across top of head using green ribbon to form leaves.

Thread Jointing

With this type of jointing, it is important to remember that threads must move freely at all times—do not stitch through the thread. Use a fine liner to mark the position on the body for arms and legs remembering to mark inside the arm and leg as well. Using a long needle and strong thread used double, insert the needle through the body at leg placement leaving long ends hanging free. Insert needle into leg slightly to the side of the pen mark exiting on other side of mark. A small stitch has been taken through the fabric and stuffing. Go back into the body just slightly away from previous stitch and exiting on other side repeating the process attaching the other leg to the body. Exit near the first stitch. Remove needle and knot all ends together securely pulling legs against the body. Thread ends on needle and bury in body stuffing. Repeat for arms.

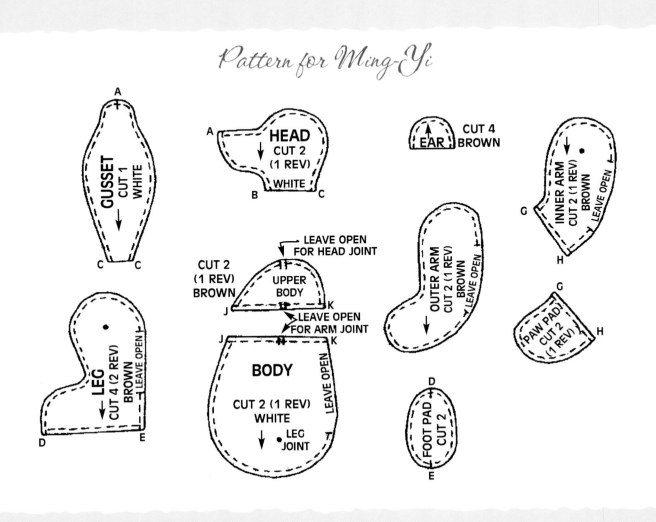

Pattern for Ming-Yi

Bea

3in (8cm). Mohair Bee Keeper bear and accessories.

The Artist
Louise Kelly—A Little Bear Business

I have enjoyed sewing and creating things all my life. In 1998, I joined the miniature club in the small seaside town where I lived and became fascinated with all small things. The following year, I made a teddy bear from a magazine. It was a very big bear, all of 10 inches (25cm) tall! I enjoyed making it very much, but it seemed more natural to try to fit bears into the miniature scenes I was enjoying at the club. So the bears became much smaller and, in the way of bears, took over completely. I now use the skills I learned there to dress and accessorize my miniature bears. I have been making and selling miniature bears and kits for the last three years and exhibit at home and in Britain four or five times a year.

Contact Details

Louise Kelly
A Little Bear Business
6 Oban Place
Westville, Durban 3630
South Africa

Tel: +27-31-262-1646
Email: lkelly@a-little-bear-business.com
Website: www.a-little-bear-business.com

Materials Needed

For Bea
- 4in x 8in (10cm x 20cm) tight backed, pre-shrunk miniature mohair (shrinking reduces the size of the mohair by approximately 10%)
- 2in (5cm) square ultra suede
- one pair 2mm onyx beads
- one 10mm cotter pin joint
- thread to match mohair
- stranded embroidery thread
- 1mm glass beads for stuffing
- polyester filling
- bear makers floss for jointing

For the net
- cocktail stick
- scrap white tulle
- thin florist's wire

For the bees
- three pipe cleaners
- six 3mm onyx or plastic beads
- yellow and black thread
- black acrylic paint
- translucent fabric (for wings)

For the Clothes
- 4in (10cm) square dark blue cotton fabric
- scrap cream cotton fabric
- scrap white cotton fabric
- 12in (31cm) each white and cream lace ½in (1cm) wide
- scrap small hole embroidery canvass for bonnet
- 8in (20cm) miniature braid
- iron on interfacing
- appliqué paper
- cotton fabric with appropriate motif (bee, flower, etc.)
- 20in (51cm) dark blue silk ribbon
- clear glue

For the hive
- aerosol can top diameter approximately 1½in (4cm)
- thick string
- glue (UHU clear)
- scrap dark brown felt or ultra suede

Special Instructions

Please refer to the miniature bear making instructions covered in the book.

Stuffing

After sewing, stuffing is the most important part of producing a professional-looking bear. You are basically sculpting the shape of your bear from the inside out, so you must never lose sight of the shape you are trying to create. Keep checking all the time that you keep the cheeks equal and the nose section firm. I have my own rather eccentric way of stuffing my bears, which I will share with you, but you may already have your own method. I take a very small amount of polyester filling and twist around my hemostats to form a small "cocoon" of hard packed stuffing. Then I slip this off the hemostats and cut it into approx. 4 small pieces. I stuff my bears very hard indeed as I find it easier to joint them and embroider the features on a firm background. The body is filled with small glass beads as well as polyester.

Fabric

Use mohair with a firm backing so that you use as little Fray Check™ as possible. I always shrink my mohair before use.

Head

Cut one center head and two side heads and a muzzle out of mohair. Cut the center head to the second line drawn across the end. Clip but do not shave the pile from the muzzle. Use the grain on the back of the mohair to ensure that the muzzle is cut out straight. Use Fray Check™ around the muzzle. I usually make a

very small puddle of Fray Check™ and apply it around the edge of the piece with a needle. You can Fray Check™ around the mohair in the same way if you wish, but too much Fray Check™ makes the pieces stiff and hard to stretch. It is necessary, however to Fray Check™ along the straight edges where you will sew the muzzle.

Sew the center head to the side heads from A to B on both sides. The first line drawn across the end of the center head is the minimum amount you can use. The more you manage to ease onto the side head, the better the shape will be.

Accuracy is very important when you are sewing the muzzle to the head.

A. Tack each end of the muzzle A to each end of the side head A.

B. Tack muzzle B to side head seam B on both sides. B is not marked on the muzzle pattern, it is just the distance from A to B on the side head. Sew from A to A, easing the muzzle from B to B across the center head.

C. Fold the muzzle in half. Mark the center. Measure 2/16in (3.18mm) on each side of the center. Mark (D). Sew from the neck edge C to D.

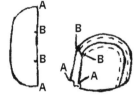

D. Flatten the top of the muzzle to form a "T" shape. Catch the center of the muzzle to D. Over sew from D to one side of the "T" and back to D. Repeat for the other side. Fasten off.

Turn right side out.

Stuff very firmly, starting with the nose, then the rest of the head. As you stuff the head, the stuffing will gradually work its way out of the nose, so you will have to continually add more stuffing to this area as you work. Try to keep the two "corners" of the nose level, as this will help you when you embroider the nose. After you have finished stuffing, it is possible to use a long darning needle to gently move the stuffing into position if you wish, but this is a technique that takes a bit of practice.

Insert the cotter pin joint. Using a double length of thread, sew a small running stitch around the neck edge

being careful not to pick up any stuffing. Insert the joint. Gently pull the thread until the neck edges fit firmly around the pin. Fasten off and cut the thread.

Position the eyes. Thread the beads onto thin pins (lace pins). You can then pin the eyes in a position that

pleases you. Generally this is just above and on the inside of the center head/muzzle seam.

Make a small mark where the pins enter the fabric. Thread your needle with a double strand of black thread (I thread the needle with both ends of the thread leaving a loop at the bottom, which I use to secure the thread.) Sew the eyes in place entering at the base of the neck and exiting at the mark you have made on the face. Thread the bead on the needle and return to the base of the neck. Return to the bead and sew through the bead again. Pull gently to sink the bead into the head. Return to the neck. Repeat once more (by this time the bead will be pretty full of thread and you may have to give it a tug to get the needle

through.) Fasten off under the head and repeat for the other eye making sure you pull the same amount so that the eyes match.

Nose

Thread your needle with two strands of brown embroidery thread. Enter at the neck and exit at one of the corners of the seam running across the nose. If you have kept the seam both straight and equal on each side (pretty unlikely – I never do,) then all you have to do is enter at the other corner of the nose seam and stitch back and forth until you have your bear's nose the size you want it. If your seam is not straight and equal, you will have to fiddle around a bit to get it right, but you do want to cover the corners of the nose seam. Rather start with the nose too small and work over the stitches to enlarge it.

Mouth

To make the mouth, enter at the side of the nose and exit at the top just under the stitches. Pull the thread through at the top and go back under the nose to the center seam (1).

Take a small stitch down the seam (approximately $3/16$ in or 5mm) (2).

Exit at the side of the face $3/16$ in (5mm) from the center seam (3).

Pull the thread through and reinsert the needle in the same place in the center seam (4).

Exit $3/16$ in (5mm) on the other side of the face at the same level as the first side (5).

Re-enter at the center seam (6) and go down to the neck and pull the thread through. Getting the two sides even can take quite a few tries, but mohair is a very forgiving fabric and allows you some mistakes without being damaged. Don't pull the thread tight or fasten off at this stage. Now that the mouth is loosely embroidered, I can spend ages pulling and adjusting the threads until I get the expression I like. Once I have achieved this, I use a small amount of Fray Check™ applied with a needle over the stitches to stabilize them. I also cover the nose with Fray Check™. Allow to dry, and then fasten off the embroidery thread. I sometimes cover the nose with a little clear nail polish to give a shine, but this is a matter of personal taste.

Body

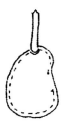

Cut out body pieces and using a single thread and a 1/16in (2mm) seam, use your needle to push the pile out of the way under the seam as you sew. Start at the top of the back and sew to the head joint markings. Insert a broken-off toothpick at the joint and sew around it so that it holds in place. This will give you a secure place to joint your bear without running the risk of poking a hole in the fabric. Sew around to the back and fasten off.

Turn right side out keeping the toothpick in place.

Jointing the Head to the Body

Remove the toothpick from the body and stick the cotter pin from the neck through the hole. Place the other disc inside the body and over the pin. Press the second disc up under the top of the body and bend the two sides of the pin slightly apart. Clip the two sides so that approximately 7/16in – 1/2in (11mm- 1cm) remains. Be careful not to cut them too short. Using your long nosed pliers, bend these in so that they coil tightly against the disc inside the body. The head should fit tightly against the body, as it will work slightly looser when you stuff the body.

Stuffing the Body

Using a small spoon, fill the body as full as you can with the glass beads.

Finish filling the body with stuffing, paying great attention to the shoulders and bottom because you will be thread jointing your bear here. I stuff my bears' bodies like a rock and they have a lovely heavy feel for such small bears, as well as being easy to joint.

Using a double thread, ladder stitch the back closed, pulling the threads tight after every few stitches. Always pull the thread downwards as pulling it to the side may rip the fabric. Carefully use your scissors to push in the edges of the fabric and the stuffing as you go. Fasten off neatly and pull the thread through the body. Cut off the thread.

Jointing the Legs

I haven't marked the place to joint the arms and legs as these can move around very easily during the stitching and stuffing. On such a small bear, it is easy to find that the marks have moved enough to give you a very lopsided look. I find that it is better to push a long pin, approximately 1/2in (1cm) from the top of each leg and pin it onto the side of the bear, about 1/2in (1cm) up from the bottom seam. Check that your bear is balanced and mark where the pin has entered at the side of the bear and the inside of each leg.

Take a length of bear makers floss and split it in two (this can be quite tricky.)

Take the thicker piece and thread it into a long darning needle.

Take one leg and pull the floss through the place you have marked on the inside to the outside of the leg. Re-enter the outside of the leg in exactly the same place and pull the floss back to the inside of the leg a few threads away. This is important or you will have a dimple on the outside of the leg when you joint the bear. Check that you haven't split the floss by pulling it gently to see that it runs freely. If it doesn't, start again, but be careful, as this will weaken the floss.

Enter the place you have marked on the side of the bear and pull the floss through to the mark on the other side. Enter the inside mark of the other leg and repeat as for the first leg.

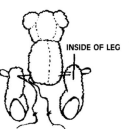

Take 2 pieces of strong string and knot one end of each to the ends of the floss (I do this because the floss is quite expensive and although you need a fairly long piece to pull, most of it is going to be cut off and thrown away).

Tie a half-knot – over and under once – between the bear and the leg.

Now you need somebody else's help.

Get them to grip the bear very tightly at the top of the legs, between their thumb and finger from the front. You need to have the threads facing you from the back. Take the threads and pull them very tightly and,

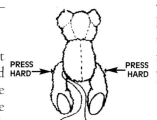

without losing the tension, complete the half-knot. Knot tightly once more and cut the threads close to the leg. Push the remaining ends gently under the leg with the point of your scissors.

DO NOT JOINT THE ARMS AT THIS STAGE

Dressing Bea
Seam allowance ¼in or 5mm

Pantaloons

1. Cut pantaloons out of white cotton.

2. Sew from A-B.

3. Iron a ⅛in–¼in (3-5mm) hem at the bottom of the legs and sew lace so just the bottom loops show. Trim off the excess lace.

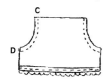

4. Sew from C-D.

5. Sew between legs E-F.

6. Turn right side out and run a small gathering thread around the bottom of the legs, just above the lace.

7. Fit the pantaloons onto Bea, pull the gathers tight around her ankles and sew the pantaloons to her ankles using small backstitches.

8. Pull the pantaloons up. You will find that they are far too long and you have to adjust them to fit. For the back, bend Bea's legs into a sitting position (if you don't do this, she will never be able to sit again), and pin the pantaloons about ½in (1cm)

down from her neck. For the front, bend her legs straight again and pin the same distance from the front of her neck. Run a gathering thread around the pantaloons, just above the pins and pull tight. Cut off the excess material and over sew the pantaloons to Bea.

Dress

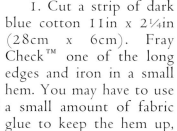

1. Cut a strip of dark blue cotton 11in x 2¼in (28cm x 6cm). Fray Check™ one of the long edges and iron in a small hem. You may have to use a small amount of fabric glue to keep the hem up, but if you do, be careful that it doesn't show on the right side. Run a hem at the top of the dress, 2in (5cm) from the bottom. Trim the hem to ¼in (5mm).

2. Sew up the back of the dress. Trim the seam, Fray Check™ and iron open. Turn right side out.

3. Using either 1 thread of Gutermann or 2 threads of any other thread, run three gathering threads around the top of the dress, one right at the top, one ¼in (5mm) below the first and one ¼in (5mm) below that. The bottom thread should be about ½in (1cm) below the first.

4. Fit the dress onto Bea. Pin the center front of the dress to the center front of the bear and the center back to the back. Pull the top thread very tight and distribute the gathers evenly. Sew the neck of the dress to the neck of the bear, being careful not to catch the head or it won't be able to turn.

5. Pull up the bottom thread and backstitch the dress to Bea's waist. Pull up the middle thread and fasten off. Pleat the gathers with your fingers so that they lie neatly.

Pinafore

1. To make the pinafore, cut a 10in x 2in (25cm x 5cm) strip of cream cotton. Fray Check™ one of the long edges and iron in a small hem. Sew the lace over the hem.

2. Iron a hem at the top of the pinafore 1in (3cm) from the bottom. Trim the hem if necessary. Sew up the back of the pinafore, trim and Fray Check™ as for the dress.

3. Run 2 rows of gathers around the top of the pinafore, one right at the top and the other just underneath. Using the second row of gathers on the dress as your guide, pin the center front of the pinafore to the center front of the dress and the center back to the back. Pull the gathers up tight and sew the pinafore to the dress.

The Arms and Sleeves

1. Take the arms you have put to one side.

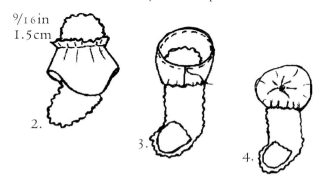

9/16in 1.5cm

2. Cut out 2 sleeves on the cross. Sew up the side seam. Run a gathering thread around the bottom of the sleeve. Fit a sleeve onto the end of each arm with the seam on the inside and the top of the sleeve pointing towards the middle of the arm. Pull the gathers up tight. Stitch the sleeve to the arm.

3. Pull the top of the sleeve up over the top of the arm. Sew the seam to the inside of the arm and run a gathering thread around the top of the sleeve.

4. Pull the gathering thread up tight and fasten off securely. Repeat for the other sleeve.

Jointing the Arms

Joint the arms in the same way as the legs, putting your needle through the dress about ½in (1cm) down from the neck. When you pull the jointing thread through the sleeve, if you go back into the same place you exited from, you won't leave a dimple when you joint your bear. Any small hole left by the thread can be closed by gently scratching the material with a needle.

Pinafore Yoke

1. To make the yoke, iron the interfacing to a piece of cream cotton. Cut around the interfacing and pin a second square of material the same size behind it. Take your yoke pattern and trace around it onto the interfacing with a water or air soluble pen (usually a blue or purple dressmakers marker.) If you are very adept with your sewing machine, you can sew around the yoke with it but I prefer to hand sew using a tiny backstitch. Cut closely around the stitching and the neck hole in the middle. Fray Check™ the neck hole and the back opening.

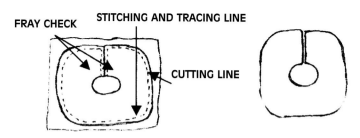

FRAY CHECK   STITCHING AND TRACING LINE

CUTTING LINE

2. Turn right side out and press flat

3. Iron appliqué paper to the back of a piece of cotton fabric with a small motif (flower, bee, etc.) and cut the motif out. Iron the motif onto the yoke.

4. Fit the yoke onto Bea. Ladder stitch the back opening. Make sure the front of the yoke is in the middle of the pinafore. Ladder stitch to the pinafore. Ladder stitch the back of the yoke to the back of the pinafore.

Bonnet

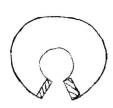

1. Iron a piece of appliqué paper the size of the bonnet brim onto a piece of dark blue cotton. Remove the paper and iron the cotton onto a piece of small hole embroidery canvas. Cut out the brim and glue braid around the edge. Overlap the center back edges and glue together.

Wendy Koutlis–Wendy Bears

My name is Wendy Koutlis and I live in Durban South Africa. I started making bears in 1995. I make miniature bears and critters ranging from 2-4in (5-10cm). I love traditional bears, but I also make character bears and animals. The penguins and ducks I make have sculpted feet and beaks made of Fimo®. I use the best quality mohair and materials available. I exhibit my bears overseas in England at the Hugglets Bear show in Kensington twice a year and have done exclusive shop signings in Germany and Switzerland. When I started making bears, I never thought that my creations would take me all over the world. I also enjoy designing my own patterns and I love to see how each new bear or critter takes on his or her own character. My bears have been in various international magazines and exclusive shop catalogues. I love making bears so much and can't think of anything better in the world to do. I have a lot of bears and monkeys in my own collection. Monkeys are my first love. I have met wonderful people from around the world and will not change my job for anything.

Contact Details

Wendy Koutlis
Wendy Bears
8 Camber Grove
10 Sarel Cilliers Crescent
Ashley, Durban, 3610
South Africa

Tel: +27-31-702 4933
Fax: +27-31-702 4933
Email: wendybears@saol.com
Website:
http://www.wendybears.homestead.com

Special Instructions

Use very sharp scissors and cut out your bear on the lines indicated on the pattern. Use a strong light-weight thread and sharp needle to sew your bear. When stitching the nose, mouth and claws, use DMC embroidery thread. Sew the bear right sides together and leave open where indicated on pattern. Turn pieces with tweezers or hemostat. Use tight backstitch when sewing your bear. Remember, small bears need small stitches.

Materials Needed

5in x 5in (13cm x 13cm) white or cream
  mohair
8in x 6in (20cm x 15cm) brown or black
  mohair
2in x 2in (5cm x 5cm) ultra suede or leather
  for foot pads
two 3mm black onyx eyes or glass eyes
polyester filling
steel pellets
five pairs of 6mm joints
six cotter pins
DMC embroidery cotton
matching thread for sewing
bees wax for nose
black or brown permanent marker
needle

Head

Using very small stitches, sew the side head pieces together from point A to B as indicated on pattern. Remember to leave open from C to B as indicated. Stitch gusset to side of head from large dot in center of snout to point C. Repeat on the other side of head. Turn head inside out. Stuff firmly by starting from the nose. Sculpt the head as you stuff .Use a double joint for head as it makes the bear more posable. Place one cotter pin through other cotter pin and insert one disc on one side. Curl ends in circular motion. That side will go in head. Run backstitch through neck opening and close neck. Push the other cotter pin through body. Attach other disc and turn in circular motion. First, place eyes to see if they are even and then sew onto bear. Pull thread tight so the eyes are embedded. Embroider nose and mouth. Use black or brown permanent marker to draw eye markings on fabric for Panda.

Ears

Sew ears together and leave open on the bottom to turn. Sew bottom opening. Attach to head by first pinning them on to see if they are well placed. Sew ears on using a ladder stitch.

Body

Sew white bottom piece of body to top brown or black body piece from A to B as indicated on pattern. Leave open where indicated and turn inside out.

Arms and Legs

Sew arm pieces together. Leave open where indicated on pattern to turn. Sew leg pieces together leaving back of leg and bottom of foot open. Place foot pad on bottom of foot and stitch in place. Turn.

To Join Limbs Using Cotter Pins and Discs

Insert joint into limb, then into body. Place second washer on inside of body. With long-nose pliers, bend cotter pin in circular motion. By now you have already attached the head as explained previously. Now you can start stuffing your bear with polyester filling. You can also use steel pellets for extra weight (steel pellets are optional and are not suitable for children.) Close openings with ladder stitching.

Nose

Use bees wax for nose. Build up a few layers of wax and then rub with plastic or cloth to get the shine effect. Hope you enjoy making Mika as much as I did.

Tips

1. When designing your bear or animal be as original a possible and try not to copy other artists.

2. People should be able to notice your bear even without a label.

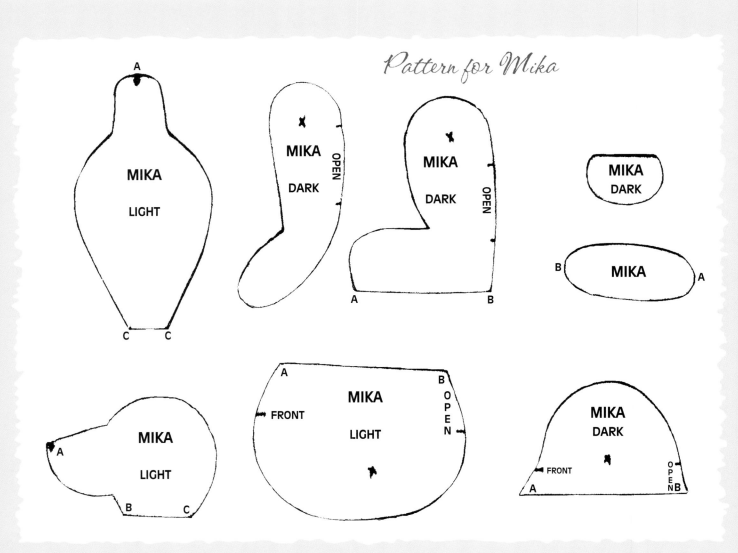

Pattern for Mika

BB (Best Bud)
6in (15cm)

Liz Walker-Watts— "Wacky" Walker Bears

My name is Liz, recently remarried with two of my own and two newly acquired teenage children. My passion for bears began when my daughter started collecting bears at the age of five; she is now twelve going on twenty. She quickly learned that the artist bears had far more character than the factory manufactured, which led to my experimentation with bear making.

Once the bear-making bug bit me, nothing could stop me, I started playing with my own designs about four years ago and enjoy this part of bear making the best. I love to see my design on paper come together in the fur. The more wacky, the more fun in the making. My biggest inspiration comes from another South African artist, Lisa Durbach, who has been a great mentor with advice on both fabrics and design. If I had one wish in life,

it would be to own every bear she has ever created. I have made bears of all sizes. Still a mad collector of other artists' kits and patterns, I always have at least one bear on the go at any given time.

I live in Westville, a suburb of Durban situated on South Africa's East coast. My inspiration for new designs comes from all forms, be it a picture in my mind, a cartoon character or a lovely piece of mohair, even a special outfit I think would look nice on a bear.

Each Walker bear is either a one-of-a-kind design or of very limited edition. My "real" Millennium collection – namely "Wacky" Walker bears – were each designed in the year 2001. Each bear carries a lucky South African penny buried deep within its stomach.

Contact Details

Liz Walker-Watts
"Wacky" Walker Bears
PO Box. 1651
Wandsbeck, 3631
Durban
South Africa

Tel: +27-31-267-1227
Fax: +27-31-267-1227
Email: lizzie@netactive.co.za

Materials Needed
8¼in x 10in (21cm x 25cm) mohair
3in x 2½in (8cm x 6cm) suede
four 10mm disks for arm joints
six 13mm disks for neck and leg joints
two cotton pins for wobbly neck joint
four T-pins for arm and leg joints
one pair 4mm black glass eyes
polyester filling
small glass beads for filling

Special Instructions
Needle Sculpture Face
Before inserting eyes by entering at eye area with needle and cotton, exit back of neck return to other eye. Pull thread taught, repeat a couple of times. This eases the strain on the glass eyes when inserted and also gives eyes a deeply set look whilst pulling the snout area upwards to create a nose bridge.

Prepare Eyes and Eyelids

As we are working on lids on such a small area, I prefer to glue the eyes on edge of the suede before cutting the eyelid out. Using strong glue, drop a dot onto half of the glass eye and carefully place on straight edge of suede. Press firmly and allow to dry before cutting out lid. Repeat for other eyelid.

Toe Sculpture Feet

Using strong thread, sculpt three toes on the tip of the foot. Once filled, cover this sculpturing using your DMC Block thread to add definition.

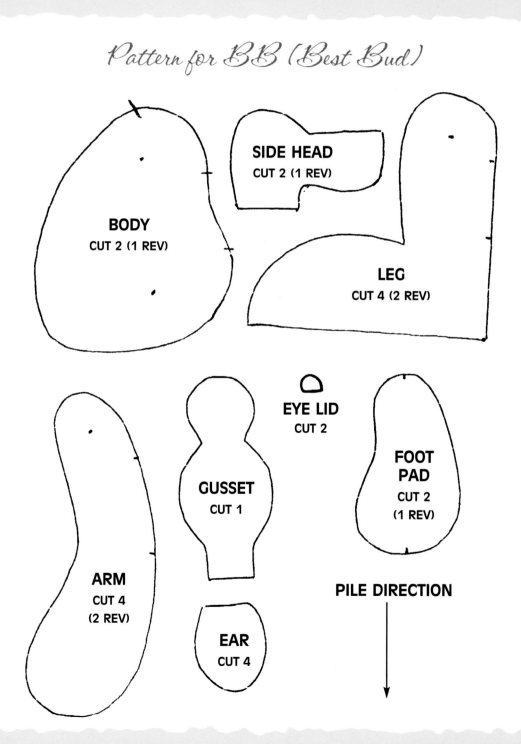

Pattern for BB (Best Bud)

BODY
CUT 2 (1 REV)

SIDE HEAD
CUT 2 (1 REV)

LEG
CUT 4 (2 REV)

EYE LID
CUT 2

FOOT PAD
CUT 2 (1 REV)

ARM
CUT 4 (2 REV)

GUSSET
CUT 1

EAR
CUT 4

PILE DIRECTION

Henry and Harry
6in (15cm). Character bear and his Hedgehog.

Michelle Neethling

I was exposed to the wonderful world of Bears many years ago. Actually as far back as my childhood really, as I never owned a doll. I was only interested in fluffy toys—teddy bears particularly. I have been an avid collector of bears for about 11 years with over 220 bears in my collection, which may not be that big, but when it comes to space, they have homes all over the house.

I have been designing and making bears myself for about 6 years. I started out by visiting our most prestigious bear shop in Johannesburg, The Bear Collection, where I had been buying bears for years. I went on my first class and was truly hooked. It really is most rewarding. I find it similar to being pregnant and giving birth all in the space of 6 to 8 hours!

I have been bringing the joy of bear making to beginners by giving classes for the past 3 years. As I mostly specialize in miniatures, I give these classes as well.

Contact Details
Mobile: +27-82-854-7877
Email: nutshell@freemail.absa.co.za

Materials Needed
matching thread for sewing together
needle
polyester filling
lead shot (optional) for weight
long-nosed pliers for turning
   cotter pins

For Henry
5in x 10in (13cm x 25cm) mustard mohair
4in x 6in (10cm x 15cm) white mohair
2¾in x 3½in (7cm x 9cm) paw pad fabric
ten 10mm disks
five cotter pins
one pair 3mm onyx eyes
thread for nose and mouth

For Harry
4in x 3in (10cm x 8cm) spiked or tipped mohair
one pair 3mm bead eyes

Special Instructions

Glue pattern pieces on cardboard and cut out to use as templates. It is always best to cut 2 pieces of each pattern where indicated to do so. Position templates on the wrong side of fabric and trace around. Take care to place the correct pattern pieces on the correct fabric, i.e. paw pads on paw pad fabric. Also take care to reverse the corresponding pattern pieces. The direction of the pile on fabric is indicated on each pattern piece.

Henry and Harry are worked entirely by hand using a backstitch. It is best to use Fray Check™ on the fabric. After tracing pattern out, Fray Check™ the whole pattern and let dry before cutting out (Fray Check™ dries in approximately 10 minutes) be careful to use a waterproof pen or a Pentel® milky pen so it does not "bleed" when Fray Check™ is applied. Perhaps use a small patch to test first. Cut out all the pattern pieces. As miniatures are so small, it is not necessary to pin and tack each piece as one would with a large bear. However the choice is up to you.

Ears
Start by joining the ear pieces. Join right sides facing. Sew from A to B leaving the bottom of the ear open.

Arms
Join the paw pads to the inner arm piece. Join A to B as indicated. Then join each arm piece together with right ides facing from C to D. Leaving an opening as indicated.

Legs
Join from A to B as indicated, and then from C to D leaving an opening as shown. The bottom of the foot is left open, as we

will be placing the foot pad in here. Now take a foot pad and mark it in 4 opposite corners (to get the exact middle, fold in half and mark, then fold in half the other way and mark.) Now pin these 4 marks to the inside of the foot. Remember to have the right side facing inside the foot and the wrong side facing you. With such a small bear it is difficult to work with pins. Therefore make 4 double stitches at each corner and remove the pins. Your footpad will be secured in place. Then complete around the footpad with a small backstitch again. You can ease in the pad from marker to marker. Be careful not to have any pleats or folds in the pad. Once this is completed, your leg is ready for turning. Carefully pinch some fabric with a hemostat, pull through the opening and turn.

Body

Join the body from A to B as indicated. Ensure enough space is left open at the back, as we will be attaching the limbs through there. Ensure markings are placed for the placing of the legs and arms. I usually use a long double thread of thick cotton, which I make quite long. Pull the cotton through and cut off so it is dangling out. Then carefully turn the body right side out. I then make a small pen dot on the fabric, as you will notice the threads can sometimes pull out and then you will have lost your mark. It is ok to make a pen mark on the right side, as the arms will cover it.

Head

Join from A to B as indicated. Then take your gusset and carefully fold in half to ensure you are getting the exact middle of the gusset. Place point A at the tip of the nose and work back from A to C. End off with a double stitch. Then go back to the front and work back from A to C. The reason for doing this is to get the gusset exactly in the middle. Cut the cotton off and turn head right side out with a hemostat.

All pieces are now sewn; turn them all out with a hemostat or similar tool. Push all seams out with a small orange stick or similar.

Jointing and Stuffing

Place a cotter pin through a disk and insert the disk through the material on the inside of the fabric, so the pin will be sticking out the material. On the right side and the disk will be on the inside. Repeat for both legs. We will be string jointing the arms, as the neck area is too small for all the cotter pins. So the arms will not have cotter pins in them. See pattern for markings for cotter pin placement. The easiest way of marking is once the arm is complete and it is turned right side out. Place the cotter pin up near the top of the arm with about 1mm from the seam. Lift the cotter pin and

place a small pen mark where the cotter pin is. Remove the cotter pin and now poke a hole where the pen mark is and insert the cotter pin went through from the inside. The disk stays inside the arm; just the silver part of the pin sticks out of the arm. You are now ready to stuff Henry. Stuff the legs first and then the arms. Ensure you fill the foot area well and then work your way up the leg. Use small pieces of stuffing at a time. Do not over stuff the limbs. Stuff up the limb and on top of the cotter pin. Do not stuff between the disk and the material. Repeat for all 4 limbs. The opening can then be closed with a ladder stitch with a strong thread.

Head

Stuff the head in the same way, starting at the nose area and working back. Once the head is filled back to the neck area, place the last disk and cotter pin in the opening. With a strong thread, tack along the opening after starting with a knot to secure the thread. Then pull on the thread and close the opening around the cotter pin. Work a few stitches to secure the thread.

Eyes

You are now ready to attach the eyes. Take a strong thread and thread it through one eye. Repeat for the other eye. Place pins in the area where you want the eyes placed. Thread the ends of the thread through a longish needle and pull through the head one at a time. Bring the needle out as close to the cotter pin at the bottom as possible. Leave the thread loose and place the other eye in the same manner. Come out very close to the first eye at the back. Tie the two pieces of cotton at the back. Hold the threads around your middle fingers, and with the head facing you, push the eyes in slightly with your thumbs while pulling at the back with your fingers. This will sink the eyes into the head. Tie tightly and bury the cotton in the head and cut off.

Ears

Pin the ears at the required place on the head and attach with a ladder stitch first across the back of the ear and then across the front. Your ears will now be secured.

Nose and Mouth

This is sewn with size 8 or 12 embroidery thread. The style of the nose you choose is a personal preference. But it is sewn in a satin stitch, very closely together. Ensure your stitches are of even length and do not pull too tightly on the thread. If I do a triangular shaped nose, I would start in the middle and then do each side, I find this helps to get a more even nose.

The mouth again is a personal choice; if you want a smiley bear then do it slightly upward, or a sad bear, slightly down. I make one long stitch and then use 2 pins to help with the placement of the V area. This ensures that the mouth is straight. Then come up to the nose again with the thread and continue with the nose. When finished with nose and mouth, bury the thread in the head and cut off.

Attaching the Limbs

You are now ready to put Henry together. Push a cotter pin through as indicated on the pattern pieces. Once the pin is sticking through into the middle, place the other disk on the inside. Curl down first one side and then the other. This should be quite tight but should still allow the limb to move freely. Repeat for all 4 limbs. Attach head in same manner. Once the legs and head are attached you can stuff the body.

You may place lead shot or glass beads in the tummy for a bit of weight. Then fill with stuffing and ladder stitch the opening at the back. Henry is finished!

Harry

Cut out both pieces of Harry as indicated, paying careful attention to the direction of the pile of his fur. Do a small backstitch from A to B as indicated. Note the shaded area on the pattern is where he will be plucked. You can either snip the hair short or pluck it out. If you choose to pluck it, first cut the white tips off, as they are glued which makes the plucking a little harder. Simply cut the white tips off and pluck out hair with tweezers.

Turn him inside out and stuff; ladder stitch closed. Thread a thread of black cotton through each eye and insert as with Henry. Come out at the underside of him, and work off. Embroider a nose and mouth as desired.

Well done. Henry and Harry are ready for a hug!

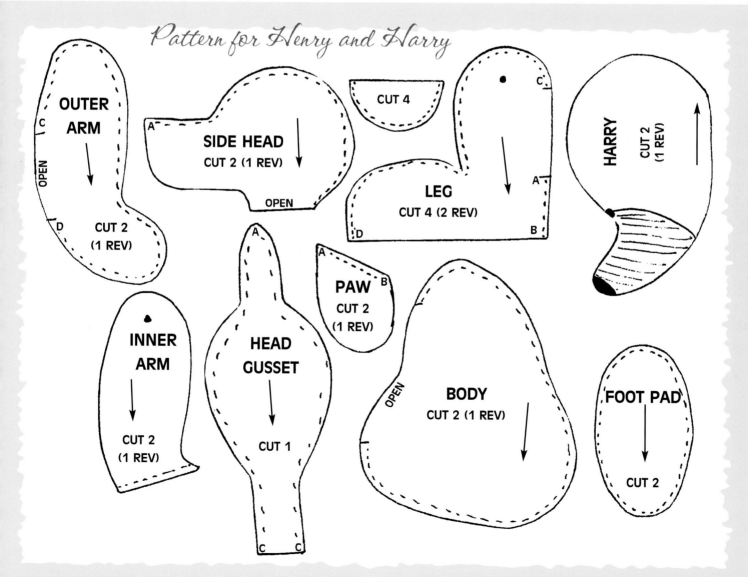

Pattern for Henry and Harry

Otto
6½in (17cm). Bear with a two-piece head and hand-knitted sweater.

The Artist
Mary-Anne Cardoso—Marylea Bears

I started making bears in 1992 when my younger son Bruce wanted a Paddington™ bear for Christmas. There weren't any available here so I realized that I was going to have to try and make one myself. I found a pattern in a magazine for the bear and then made and dressed it myself. I really enjoyed making the bear so I made more and more until my mother suggested that I take a table at a craft market. I did and sold the bears and also got more orders. At that time, mohair and other synthetics weren't available so I used anything that I thought would look nice for a bear. I then progressed onto doing my own designs. I don't do the craft markets anymore, but do a few bear fairs during the year. The first bear fair I did was in 1993 in Durban and I have been attending them ever since. At the fair in 1994, I entered my first competition and was awarded 1st place in the dressed bear category. I have entered the competition every year since then and have managed to win awards each time. I particularly enjoy the challenge of doing the dressed bear, but I also like the undressed ones because some mohair just shouldn't be covered up. Unfortunately, I haven't had the opportunity to attend any overseas bear fairs yet, but still hope to someday. I call my bears "Marylea Bears." Mary being the first part of my name and Lea being the first part of my maiden name, which was Leach.

Contact Details

Mary-Anne Cardoso
Marylea Bears
14 Allan Hirst Drive
Northern Park
Pietermaritzburg, 3201
South Africa

Tel: +27-33-342-8414
Cell: 082-644-8785
Email: maryanne@iafrica.com

Materials Needed

fat ¹/₁₆in mohair
4in x 2¾in (10cm x 7cm) piece of ultra suede
one pair of 6mm black glass eyes
five sets of 15mm fiber joints and five cotter pins
thread to match mohair
DMC no. 8 perle embroidery thread for nose
strong thread for inserting the eye

Special Instructions
Head

With right sides together, stitch from the front neck (A) to the back neck (B). Turn the head the right side out and stuff firmly, especially the nose area. Place a disk on a cotter pin and insert the disk in the neck. Gather up neck and secure thread so that it won't come undone.

Body

Sew the darts in the two body pieces at the neck and crotch area. Then with right sides together, stitch the two body pieces in place leaving the opening where indicated and a very small opening at the top for the neck joint.

Tips

Use felt and cut it to the nose shape that you like. Backstitch it into position. Then embroider over the template with satin stitching. If you run your thread through bee's wax before using it, it will prevent the thread from tangling. Additional wax can be rubbed on the nose afterwards and then buffed with paper or a soft cloth to give a more realistic look.

Otto's Sweater

Instructions

Cast on 28 stitches in main color and knit rib (K1, P1) for 4 rows.

Rows 1 & 2: Knit 2 rows in contrast color.

Rows 3 to 6: Stocking stitch (K1 row, P1 row) (4 rows).

Repeat rows 1 to 6 once more and then rows 1 & 2 once again.

Keeping colors in sequence:

Knit 2 together, knit to last 2 stitches, knit 2 together.

Knit 1 row.

Continue decreasing every alternate row until 10 stitches remain. Place stitches on spare needle.

Knit 3 more pieces the same placing them onto the same spare needle.

Neck:

You will have 40 stitches on the spare needle. Knit these in K1, P1 rib for 6 rows.

Cast off loosely and sew up the sweater.

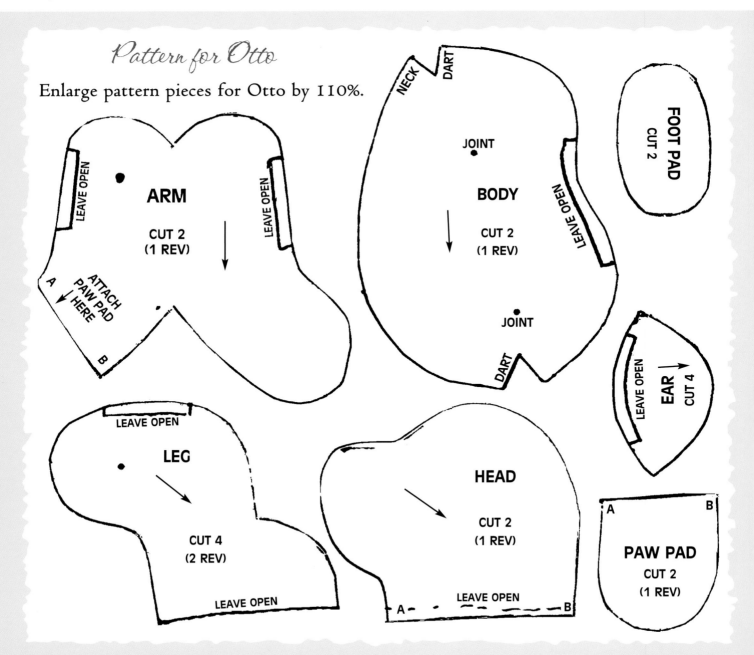

Pattern for Otto

Enlarge pattern pieces for Otto by 110%.

ARM
CUT 2
(1 REV)

LEAVE OPEN

ATTACH PAW PAD HERE
A
B

NECK
DART

JOINT

BODY
CUT 2
(1 REV)

LEAVE OPEN

JOINT

DART

FOOT PAD
CUT 2

LEAVE OPEN

EAR
CUT 4

LEAVE OPEN

LEG
CUT 4
(2 REV)

LEAVE OPEN

HEAD
CUT 2
(1 REV)

LEAVE OPEN

A   B

A   B

PAW PAD
CUT 2
(1 REV)

Persephone
6½in (17cm). Goddess of Spring.

The Artist

Elin Anstey–Elimae Bears

After a trip to California in 1997 where I couldn't find a bear that wasn't made in China, I came home and found *Threadbears,* a bear-making supplies store here in Durban, South Africa. That was the start of my bear making career. I really love it and it's improved so much since I started designing my own bears. I would rather make a bear than do anything else. Fortunately, my husband, Adrian and son, Daniel, don't seem to mind. The two Dalmatians also seem to cope well, although Jazz, the eldest, gets upset when he's not allowed to kiss the newest creation. I would love to read more about the bears I cherish, but at this point in my bear making career, I am fortunate enough to be in a position where I'm continuously busy with orders for collectors, stores and shows. Perhaps someday I'll get the opportunity.

Contact Details

Elin Anstey
Elimae Bears
7 Pelican Place
Illovo Glen
Kwa Zulu Natal, 4126
South Africa

Phone: +27 (0) 31-916-4721
Email: Antline@freemail.absa.co.za

Special Instructions

Please refer to the general bear making instructions covered in the book.

Head

Pin the head pieces fur sides together. Sew along the jaw from nose to neck. With the right sides together, pin the gusset to the head pieces. Pin, easing gusset around the head. Sew from the center nose to the back of the neck on both sides. Turn your headpiece right side out. Using filling of your choice, stuff firmly. This is a very important part of your bear, so stuff slowly from the snout shaping the head as you go along. Using a double piece of strong thread, sew a row of gathering stitches around the neck edge. Insert a T-pin joint, pull ends tight, knot, and bury threads.

Assembling and Stuffing

Take the head piece and insert the shank of the T-pin through the top of the body where indicated. Insert a disk and bend T-pin to secure. Repeat for arms and legs joining in the same manner using disks and T-pin's. Ensure that each joint is finished off tightly as they will loosen up a little as you stuff your bear. Once stuffed, sew the openings together using a ladder stitch.

Eyes

Experiment with eye placement as this also plays an important part of your finished bear's expression. Using a strong double thread, thread through each eye shank, center thread and knot leaving tails of thread. Using pliers, gently squeeze the wire eye loops around the thread to form a stem on the back of the eye. Repeat for other eye. Thread tails of one eye through your long doll needle and poke it through eye

---

Materials Needed

1/8 yard/meter mohair of your choice
four 17mm joints
six 13mm joints
7 or 8mm eyes
ultra suede for footpads
filling of your choice
embroidery thread of your choice for nose and
  nails

placement mark. Bring your needle out at the base of the back of the head. Do not tie off. Repeat for other eye bringing your thread out beside the other threads. Tie these threads into a knot pulling in the eyes as you do so. Now thread all the threads onto your long needle and thread back into the head to loose the threads. Cut off the excess cotton.

Nose

Trim down a triangle of fur on the end of the muzzle approximately where you are going to stitch the nose. You may wish to use a template by cutting the shape of your nose out of a small piece of black felt and tacking it in place. Using pearl thread, satin stitch nose and mouth. Needle sculpture facial features to give your bear personality.

Pattern for Persephone

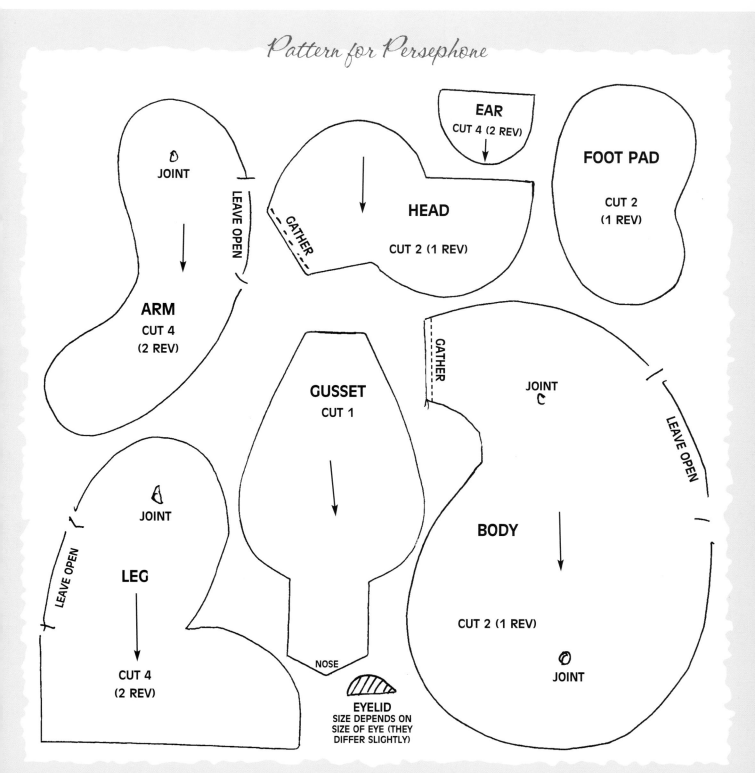

Tyler
6in (15cm). Fully-jointed bear.

The Artist

Jenny Tomkins–Jenny Bears

I love sewing and bears are my passion, especially miniatures! I am the ultimate arctophile! I love bringing different little personalities to life and become very attached to my creations, often finding it difficult to part with them! It is very rewarding however, to see the pleasure on other peoples' faces as they purchase one of my bears to add to their family. I've resided in Durban, on the East Coast of South Africa for most of my life with my husband of 28 years, Frank. I mainly make miniatures and character bears, which is definitely where my talent lies. All are hand-stitched, and each one has its own facial expression and personality. I have also made golliwogs and other animals such as cats, dogs, horses, penguins, rabbits, kangaroos and elephants. Anything goes, as I love a challenge! For inspiration, I look through children's storybooks and greeting cards. Bear making is more than just a hobby to me – it has become a large part of my life and it is extremely satisfying. I can't think of anything I'd rather be than a bear artist, and I find it personally rewarding after each and every bear I bring to life.

Contact Details

Jenny Tomkins
Jenny Bears
3 The Oaks, Albion Place
Morningside, 4001
Durban
South Africa

Tel: +27-31-303-3070
Email: Jennybears_za@hotmail.com
Website: www.jennybears.co.za

Materials Needed

9in x 13½in (23cm x 34cm) sparse mohair, which includes footpads that are clipped or shaved (ultra suede can be used instead but has to match fabric as paw pads are shaved as well)
ten hardboard discs 10mm
six small cotter pins (extra one allows for wobble head)
marking pen for tracing pattern pieces cut from cardboard onto fabric
scissors
hemostat for turning pieces right side out.
needle
black embroidery thread for nose, mouth and claws
matching thread for fabric used for body
polyester filling
glass beads
two 3mm black onyx beads or glass eyes on wire
scraps of wool for knotting patches or scarf

Special Instructions

Please refer the general bear making instructions covered in the book.

Allow about ¼in or 5mm seam allowances to prevent unraveling. Tuck the fur in as you sew.

Body

Sew darts first and then assemble as usual.

Arms

Clip or shave fur from paw of inner arm pieces. Sew around arm leaving opening for turning.

Wobble Joint

Splay the ends of one cotter pin and slip one of the ends into the loop of another cotter pin so that they are joined through their loops. Insert a disc over one of the cotter pins with a washer and secure by turning with a cotter pin turner or pliers. Then use as normal for the neck joint.

Stuffing

Pour glass beads using a small funnel into bottom half of body. Stuff rest of body with polyester filling then stitch seam using ladder stitch. Stuff arms and legs - glass beads first, then stuff firmly with polyester and ladder stitch openings.

Eyes

Trim fur from muzzle, (I prefer to clip the area) but be careful not to pull a thread. Using a single strand of floss (nylon thread) insert at eye placement, and exit at the base of back of head. Pull securely and knot. Before cutting, insert to other side of head, then cut thread. Repeat with other eye.

Nose and Mouth

Using a single strand of embroidery thread, stitch nose using vertical satin stitch. Then stitch mouth. Use Tyler's photograph as a guideline.

Claws

Insert needle threaded with embroidery cotton, at side of paw or foot. Sew three vertical stitches from toe to top of foot.

Accessories

Patches - c/o 5 stitches garter/stitch 4 rows, c/off. Sew onto chest of bear, using black thread. **Bows/scarves** - c/o 8 stitches in crochet cotton, garter stitch to desired length. C/off, tie around bear's neck. (or just put a bell around the neck to finish off your bear.)

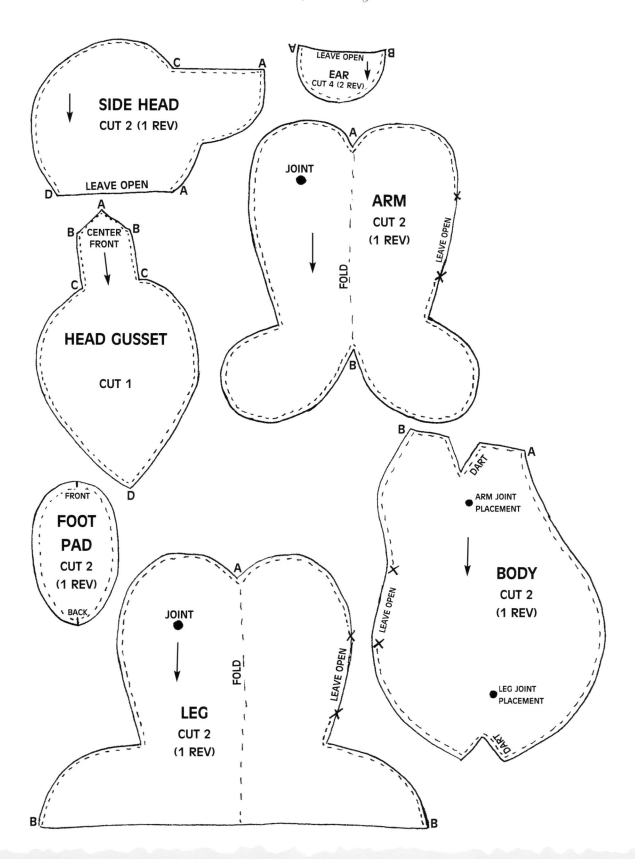

Pattern for Tyler

SIDE HEAD
CUT 2 (1 REV)

LEAVE OPEN

EAR
CUT 4 (2 REV)

ARM
CUT 2
(1 REV)

JOINT

FOLD

LEAVE OPEN

CENTER
FRONT

HEAD GUSSET

CUT 1

FOOT
PAD
CUT 2
(1 REV)

FRONT

BACK

LEG
CUT 2
(1 REV)

JOINT

FOLD

LEAVE OPEN

BODY
CUT 2
(1 REV)

DART

ARM JOINT
PLACEMENT

LEAVE OPEN

LEG JOINT
PLACEMENT

DART

Punkie Panda
6½in (17cm). Panda bear with "a difference".

The Artist

Carol Casey—Caz Bears

Dare to be different is my motto. Yes, traditional bears have their place in the market, but I like unusual bears, and that is what I like to make. They must make you smile, laugh and forget all your troubles even if for just a moment. I started making bears in August 1995 quite by accident. My sister asked me to join her in a class, as she didn't want to go on her own. I have always loved all forms of sewing—there just had to be a needle involved and I was hooked. I always thought teddy bears were for children, so I was surprised at myself when bears began to take over my life.

I started making bears in synthetic fur, as that was all that was available in South Africa until I contacted a friend in London and she sent me some mohair. I now hand-dye, tie-dye and paint mohair. There is no end to the rainbow of beautiful mohair that is available, but coming up with a new color is part of the joy of bear making with "a difference."

I soon started entering competitions and over the years have received many awards in South Africa.

After nearly 7 years in this wonderful business, I now have bears in America, Canada, England, Switzerland, Germany, Singapore, Australia and many in South Africa. I have been designing patterns to sell for a number of years and have a faithful following of bear makers eagerly anticipating what's next. I would like to take this opportunity to say a very big thank you to all the collectors all over the world for encouraging me to be "different." I also want to thank the Lord from the bottom of my heart for giving me the talent, providing funds, and for His many blessings that I have received from the collectors and bear makers.

Contact Details
Mobile: +27-82-572-1383

Materials Needed
10in x 6in (25cm x 15cm) black mohair
8in x 6in (20cm x 15cm) white mohair
4½in x 2½in (12cm x 6cm) ultra suede
1½in x 1½in (4cm x 4cm) long pile mohair
one pair 5mm glass eyes
one set 13mm mini joints
heavy-duty thread in white and black
polyester filling
100 Grams glass beads (optional)
black fabric marker or permanent marker

Special Instructions

Please refer to the general bear making instructions covered in the book. Cut out all pattern pieces and place onto cardboard. Trace all pieces onto the correct colors of mohair, reversing where necessary. Cut out carefully. The pieces can be sewn on a machine or by hand, but the complete head and pads should be sewn by hand using a tiny backstitch. When he is finished, make him an ultra suede waist coat, and add some chains or what ever accessories you want.

Head

Join the head gusset pieces as follows. Pin and sew "A" to "B" and "C" to "D". The long pile mohair must be in the center of the gusset. Now pin and sew the two side head pieces together from neck edge to nose tip. Pin and sew head gusset, easing in where necessary. Turn carefully. Stuff head making sure the nose area is firm for easy embroidery. Make sure he has well-defined cheeks and forehead. Place joint in place and close opening securely.

Body

Using the correct color threads, sew darts in lower body. Pin and sew lower body to upper body—"A" to "B". Place the pieces together, matching all seams. Pin and sew, leaving open where indicated. Turn.

Ears

Pin and sew around curve. Repeat for other ear. Turn straight edge in and ladder stitch closed using strong thread. Do not cut thread. Pin into desired position on head and ladder stitch to head. Place earring in one ear if desired when he is completed.

Jointing and Stuffing

Joint head at mark on inner body. Joint arms and legs at markings on inner body. Make sure joints are tight. Place glass filling in lower body and fill up with stuffing. Close, using a ladder stitch.

Eyes, Nose and Mouth

Sculpt eye area if desired. Using a black fabric marker, mark eye patches and insert eyes in usual manner. Embroider nose and mouth.

Punkie Panda Waistcoat

Materials Needed

6½in x 4½in (17cm x 12cm) ultra suede
silver beads
lots of imagination

Carefully trace out the back and front. Cut out inside the lines so that no markings show.

Sew back to font at shoulders and then at the sides.

Place waistcoat on Punkie Panda and sew silver bead to close waistcoat.

Now use your imagination and add chains or anything else that takes your fancy.

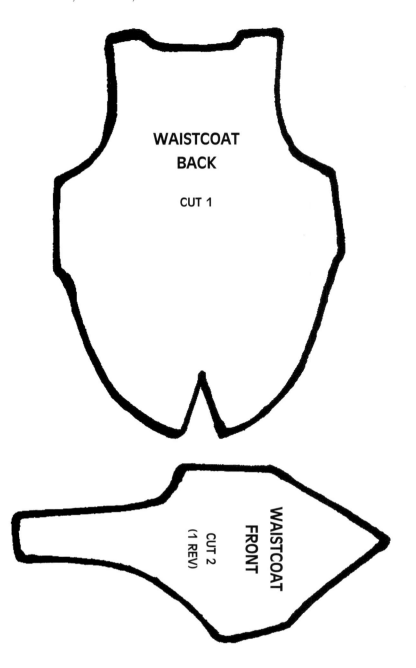

WAISTCOAT BACK

CUT 1

WAISTCOAT FRONT

CUT 2 (1 REV)

Pattern for Punkie Panda

ULTRA SUEDE

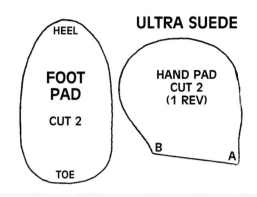

HEEL

FOOT PAD

CUT 2

TOE

HAND PAD
CUT 2
(1 REV)

B A

LONG PILE

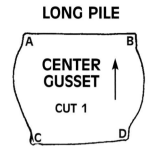

A B

CENTER GUSSET

CUT 1

C D

BLACK MOHAIR

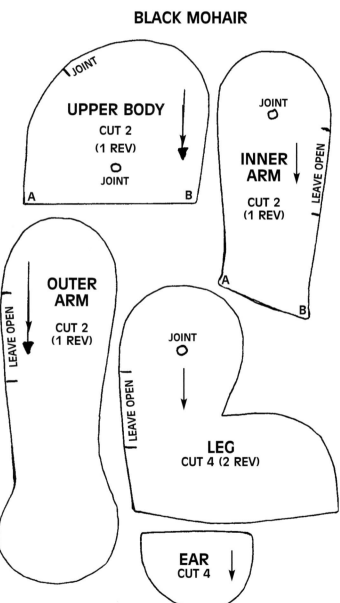

JOINT

UPPER BODY

CUT 2
(1 REV)

JOINT

A B

JOINT

INNER ARM

CUT 2
(1 REV)

LEAVE OPEN

A

B

OUTER ARM

CUT 2
(1 REV)

LEAVE OPEN

LEAVE OPEN

JOINT

LEG
CUT 4 (2 REV)

EAR
CUT 4

WHITE MOHAIR

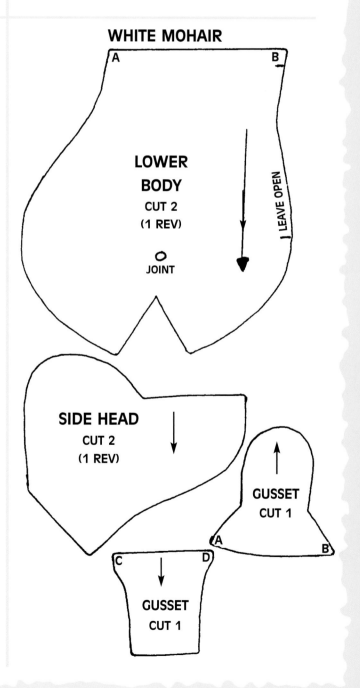

A B

LOWER BODY

CUT 2
(1 REV)

JOINT

LEAVE OPEN

SIDE HEAD

CUT 2
(1 REV)

GUSSET
CUT 1

A B

C D

GUSSET
CUT 1

Colette
8in (20cm). Loosely jointed bear.

The Artist

Di Sturgess–Teddytech

I learned to sew as a child and my fascination with various textiles fuelled my interest in dress designing in the 1970's, quilt making in the 1980's and finally bear making in the 1990's! I have a BA degree (Communication and Psychology) and enjoy imparting my knowledge and sharing my bear making skills with others. As a teacher, my goal is to instill confidence and unlock the creative and artistic potential in my students.

In addition to exhibiting my bears at fairs in England, the USA and Germany, in 1993, I initiated Durban's Annual Teddy Bear & Doll Fair, held in conjunction with a Bearmaker's Competition. The purpose was to encourage bear makers to promote and sell their bears, to improve the standard of bear making, and raise awareness among the general public thus stimulating an interest in arctophily. Funds are raised at each fair and then donated to The Reach for a Dream Foundation.

Contact Details
Tel: +27-31-312-7755
Fax: +27-31-312-9564
Email: ebeaton@global.co.za

Special Instructions
Please refer to the general bear making instructions covered in the book.

Loose Jointing
When securing the nut and bolt joints, do not tighten them as normal. This allows for a really floppy beanbag feel and makes posing your bear a pleasure.

Materials Needed
1/16 in yard/meter mohair fabric
3½in x 3in (9cm x 8cm) ultra suede for paw pads
one pair 6mm glass eyes
ten 20mm discs
one cotter pin and two washers for neck joint
four lock nuts
four bolts
eight washers
black No.8 DMC perle cotton for embroidering nose and claws

Pattern for Colette

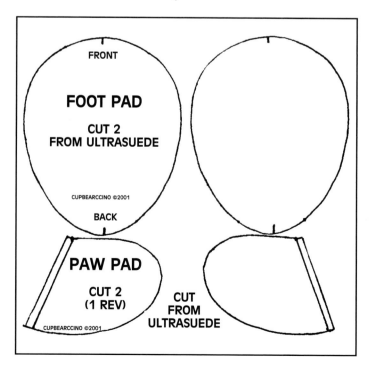

FRONT

FOOT PAD
CUT 2
FROM ULTRASUEDE

CUPBEARCCINO ©2001

BACK

PAW PAD
CUT 2
(1 REV)

CUPBEARCCINO ©2001

CUT FROM ULTRASUEDE

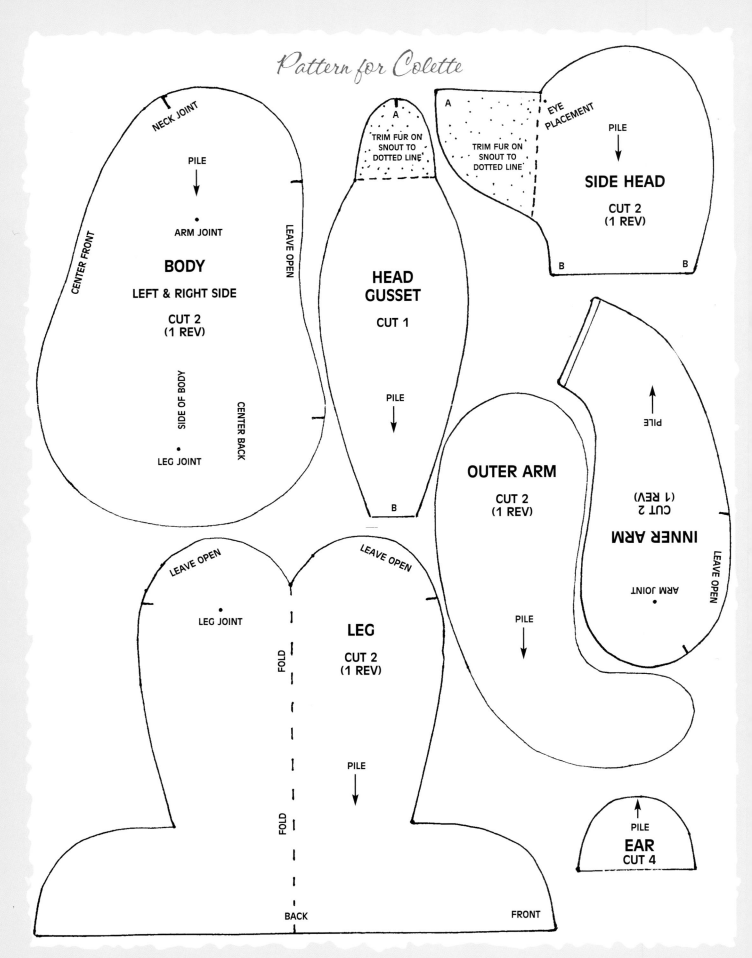

Zimba

10in (25cm). Fully-jointed bear with shaded face detail.

The Artist

Janet Changfoot-Changle Bears

I have been making bears for the past 6 years and exhibit locally as well as internationally several times a year. I was the winner of the British Bear Artist Award 2000. I sell to collectors and specialist shops worldwide.

Every Changle Bear is a collector bear made from the finest quality German or English mohair. All are fully jointed and have glass eyes. Each bear features airbrushed detail, which enhances the imaginative designs giving the bears a unique look and lovable come-alive appearance.

Changle Bears are made in small limited editions or are one-of-a-kind. They are made with love, extreme care and attention to detail. Changle Bears already have homes worldwide and you are invited to look at the latest bears available for adoption on my website.

Contact Details

Janet Changfoot
Changle Bears
71 Vincent Gardens North
Vincent
East London 5247
South Africa

Tel: +27- 43-726-9331
Fax: +27-43-743-1130
Email: footman@intekom.co.za
Website: www.changlebears.co.za

Materials Needed

1/8 yard/meter mohair
five 35mm hardboard cotter pin joints
one pair 10mm black glass eyes
No. 5 black perle thread for nose
ultra suede for pads
strong thread for closing and inserting eyes
awl
polyester filling
plastic pellets

Special Instructions

Read all instructions carefully before you begin.

Trace out the pattern onto cardboard and cut out before you begin.

Place the pattern pieces onto the wrong side of the fabric being careful to make sure the fur pile is in the direction of the arrows on the pattern pieces. Draw around the pattern pieces copying all the markings as indicated for joints, etc.

Using material for pads, trace and cut out paw pads

When cutting out, remember to be careful not to cut the fur pile but only the backing. It is preferable to trim away a small amount of the fur pile from edge of pieces to give clean seams once stitched.

All pieces should be pinned and preferably tacked before sewing. ¼in to 5mm seams are allowed.

Abbreviations: RST - right sides together, RSO - right sides out.

Body

RST sew darts on body pieces. Pin and tack body pieces together leaving open as indicated. Sew.

Arms

RST pin and tack paw pad to inside arm pieces. Sew. RST pin and tack outside arm pieces to inside arm pieces leaving open as indicated. Sew.

Legs

RST pin and tack leg pieces leaving open at bottom and back as indicated. Sew. RST tack footpad to bottom of leg matching center toe and heel. Sew.

Ears

RST pin and tack ears together leaving bottom open. Sew. Turn RSO and ladder stitch closed. Turn all body pieces RSO.

Head

RST pin and tack side head pieces together from A to B. Sew. Secure head gusset at tip of nose with a couple of stitches. Pin and tack head gusset from A to C on each side. Sew. Bottom should be open for stuffing. Turn RSO. Stuff head well with small pieces of stuffing making sure the nose is especially firm. Shape the head as you stuff. Once the head is firmly stuffed, run a gathering stitch around the neck edge with strong thread or floss. Place one wooden joint with washer and cotter pin in the head opening, shank out and pull up threads tightly, tie off tightly and lose thread in head. Cut off thread.

Make a small hole in the top on the body with an awl. Push shank through. On the inside of the body, add a wooden joint and washer and curl cotter pin back tightly with pliers.

Jointing Limbs

With an awl poke a small hole in the inside of the arms and legs as indicated. Insert the joint (disc, washer and cotter pin) through the hole. Make a small hole with the awl in the corresponding body area as marked and push the shank of the cotter pin through from the outside. On the inside of the body, slip on the disc and washer and curl the pin back with needle point pliers the same way as with the head joint. Make sure the joints are as tight as possible.

Stuffing

Stuff the arms and legs firmly. Close the limbs with ladder stitch. Stuff the body with either polyester filling or a mixture of stuffing and pellets. Close body opening with ladder stitch.

Ears

Using pins, position the ears as desired and sew in place with ladder stitch all round.

Nose

Patience and practice are needed for a good nose so begin with an easy shape. Trim the fur away from the bear's face as desired, but leave the nose area especially clean. Use perle thread in preferred color. Choose either a triangular or rectangular nose for a beginner; sew an inverted V or Y for the bear's mouth.

Glass Eyes

Once you have decided on the position of the eyes by using glass headed pins, make a small hole with an awl. Thread a length of floss or strong thread onto the glass eye and pinch the wire loop closed. Thread onto a long doll needle and pushing it through the hole made for the eye, come out in the middle of the neck just above the head joint. Leave the two threads hanging at the back. Repeat for the other eye coming out a couple of mm's away from the first threads. Make sure the eye loop has gone into the bear's head. Tie off firmly with several knots and lose the thread in the head.

Brush all trapped fur from seams.

Optional Highlighting

I use an airbrush technique to highlight my bear's face, which is too difficult to explain in the pages of this book. You can however use fabric pens such as Marvey® pens or similar which are available in many beary colors to highlight behind the bear's eyes (before setting the eyes) around the nose and ears if you wish.

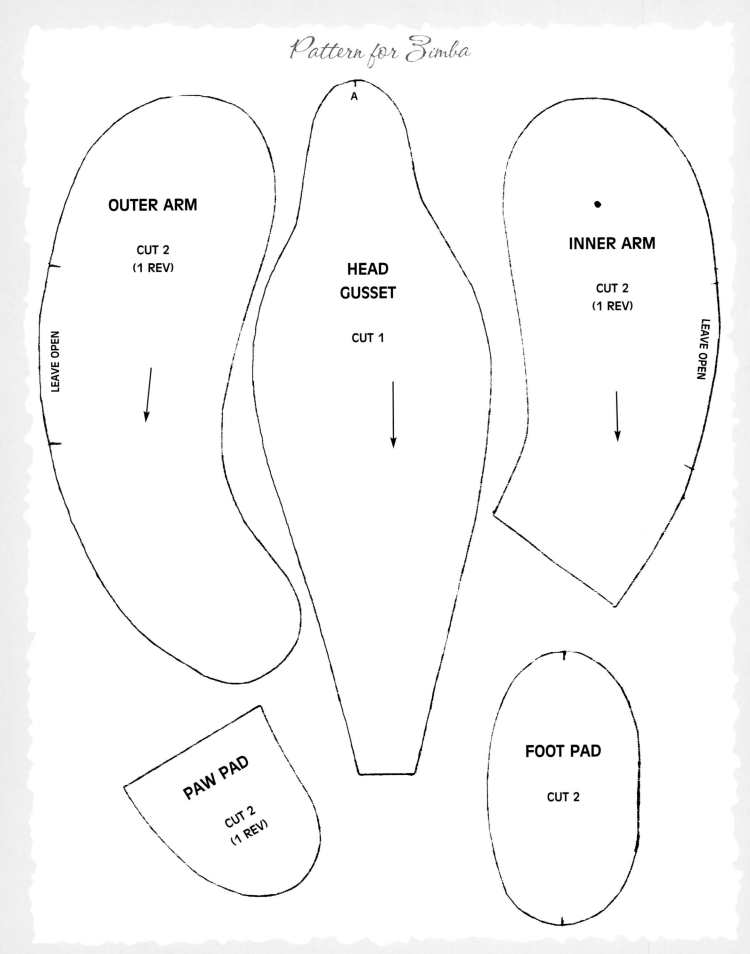

Pattern for Zimba

A

OUTER ARM

CUT 2
(1 REV)

LEAVE OPEN

**HEAD
GUSSET**

CUT 1

INNER ARM

CUT 2
(1 REV)

LEAVE OPEN

PAW PAD

CUT 2
(1 REV)

FOOT PAD

CUT 2

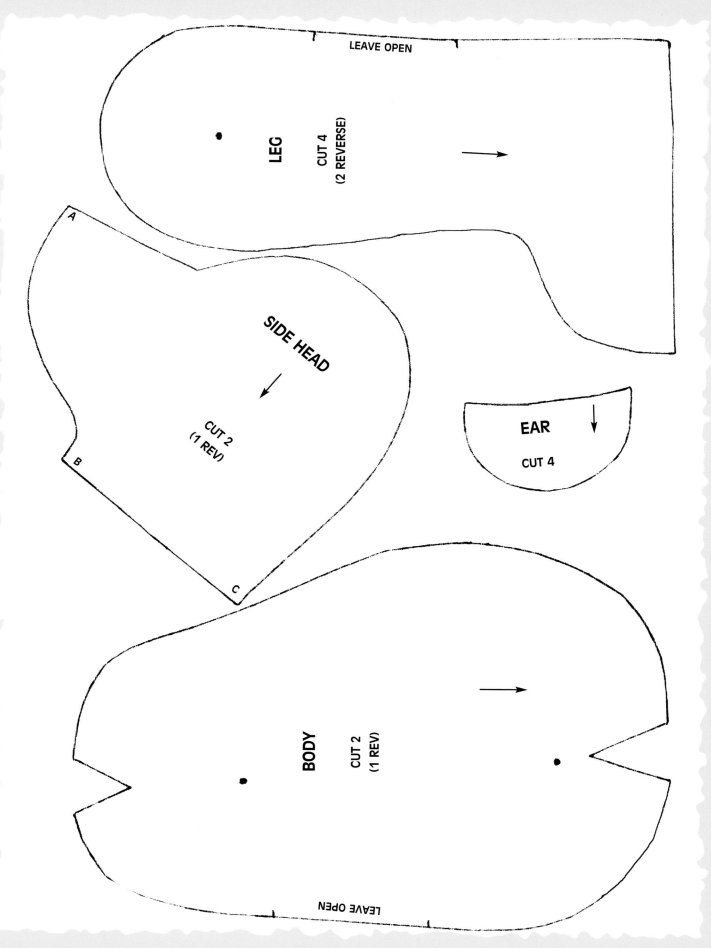

LEAVE OPEN

LEG

CUT 4
(2 REVERSE)

A

SIDE HEAD

CUT 2
(1 REV)

B

C

EAR

CUT 4

BODY

CUT 2
(1 REV)

LEAVE OPEN

83

Fran

10in (25cm). Patchwork bear fully jointed.

The Artist

Lisa Durbach—Scruff Bears

I made my first bear, Miro, in 1996 and I began selling them in 1997. Pauline Cockrill's *Teddy Bear Encyclopedia* inspired me. I read it through from cover to cover.

I completed a National Diploma in Theatre Arts focusing on props and décor painting. It also included six months of costume construction. I then did my B-tech in puppetry. I began my working career at a company that made puppets, props, décor, costumes and make-up for children's television in South Africa. There I was fortunate enough to meet Nelson Mandela, however, I don't think he would recognize me now as I was in a bright green monster suit at the time. This put a sparkle in my bear making wrist for years to come.

Since then, I have been traveling in the UK and becoming a world famous bear and animal artist. I had the wonderful opportunity to work for and with Barbara and Andy at Barbara-Ann bears who are award-winning British bear artists. There they worked me like a "dawg" (a word Barbara and Andy used for their treatment of me, apparently it means dog.) I attended several bear fairs including the Hugglets fairs in Kensington and Teddybar Total in Munster. It's always good to meet the people who collect my crazy creations. I have appeared in many top international magazines in addition to this book. I've sold bears to many of the best shops and I am featured in various bear shop catalogues (such as Teddy Bears of Witney.) I have also had the privilege of exhibiting my bears, animals and dolls at a top South African art gallery. I have won many awards in South Africa and most recently won a 2nd prize in the bear of the year competition on the Planet Teddy Bear website (www.planet-teddybear.com). I was the October artist of the month with the vote for artist of the year in October.

I have an overactive imagination and an interest in cartoons and animation, which is why most of my work looks like it could have hopped off a television or cinema screen. My work is contemporary, whimsical, adventurous and always pushing the boundaries. I don't set any limits on what I should do. If I think it's a good idea, I'll go ahead and make it. I always want to try something new and don't particularly enjoy repeating the same idea. I love working with colored dyes and pens and combining bits of mohair on a single bear; hence my inspiration for Fran.

Fran was used as a class friendship project at the Tin Soldiers Studio in Pretoria. Every person in the class added to each other's patchwork. In the end, each student had enough patchwork to make their own Fran.

Lisa Durbach
Scruff Bears
171 River Valley rd
Lynwood Glen, 0081
Pretoria
South Africa

Contact Details

Tel: +27-12-348-4399
Email: durbach@iafrica.co.za
or: durbachlisa@hotmail.com
Website: http://www.angelfire.com/sc2/scruffzoo/

Special Instructions
Making the Patchwork Fabric

Look at the scraps you have. Choose the colors that compliment one another, i.e. all browns and yellows, etc. Do not use colors that are too much of a contrast to the rest. If you want, you can make the whole patchwork piece, and then dye the whole piece so that all the colors will match. Disregard the direction of the fur pile for this bear because you are going to trim all the hair off. Choose a size scrap that is comfortable for you to work with and try to keep the size consistent. Start with two pieces (use unusual shapes when possible.) Make sure that both have one straight side, and then sew it together. Continue sewing more pieces together. Cut the pieces straight if necessary.

Where two or more pieces form a shape, cut that shape from the scraps, and sew it in place. You can machine sew when there is just one side, but hand sew with tight stitches, when more than one side is involved. Please feel free to experiment with colors, shapes and sizes.

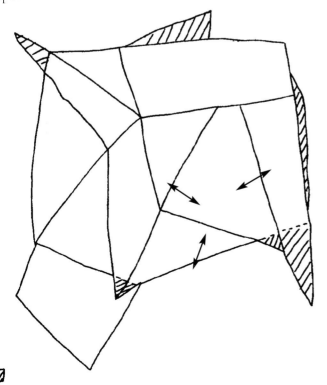

Piece cut off. Try using interesting shapes.

Making the Bear

Lay the material as flat as possible, and draw out the pattern pieces as indicated on the pattern. Cut the pieces out, and sew the pieces with the fur on the inside. Then turn the pieces to face outwards. Stuff the arms, legs, head and body with the tiny scraps of mohair. This gives the bear a solid weight. Then you can really say that you waste no mohair! Close the body parts with a ladder stitch.

Cut the bear's muzzle from a neutral color, like beige or cream, and then trim the fur. Sew along the seam line shown and then stuff the muzzle with polyester filling, but don't stuff it solid. Sew the bear's muzzle onto the face with a contrasting thread.

Sew a nose on with any fabric, and embroider over it. Then embroider a smile.

Sew the ears, so that the hairless piece is facing outwards. Close up the bottom with a blanket stitch. Pin the ears to the head and ladder stitch it to the head.

Tie the floss to the loop of the eye. Squash the loop with your pliers. Thread each floss separately, both entering the same hole, but each strand must exit just behind the ear a tiny distance apart. Tie the floss.

Attach the head to the body by using a blanket stitch. Sew the limbs securely to the body, but make sure that it can move easily.

Embroider hand and feet claws. You can also embroider other decorative stitches to the bear.

Don't worry about symmetry. The imperfection adds to the character of the bear.

Attaching the Limbs

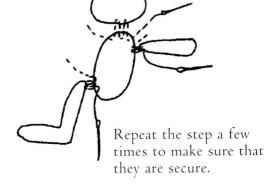

Repeat the step a few times to make sure that they are secure.

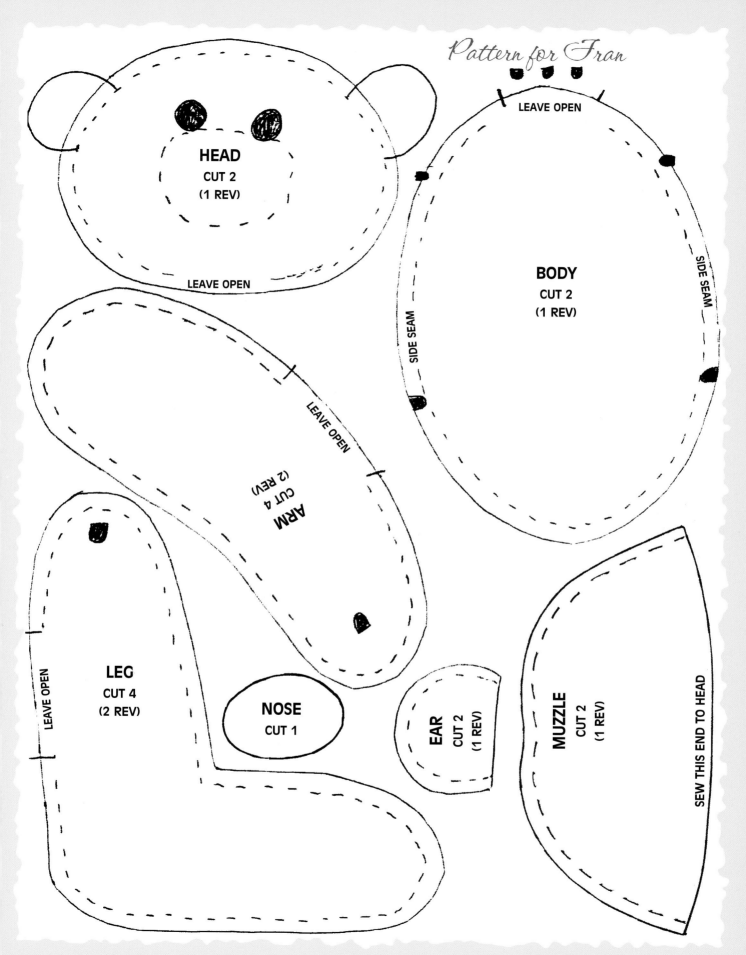

Pattern for Fran

HEAD
CUT 2
(1 REV)

LEAVE OPEN

BODY
CUT 2
(1 REV)

LEAVE OPEN

SIDE SEAM

SIDE SEAM

LEAVE OPEN

ARM
CUT 4
(2 REV)

LEG
CUT 4
(2 REV)

LEAVE OPEN

NOSE
CUT 1

EAR
CUT 2
(1 REV)

MUZZLE
CUT 2
(1 REV)

SEW THIS END TO HEAD

Gabbey

12in (31cm).
Traditional bear with accessories.

The Artist

Lynette Kennedy–Fred-I-Bear

I started making teddy bears to keep busy after selling my needlecraft business and when both children grew up and were busy with their own lives. What started off as a hobby has now turned into full-time business. I trade under the name of "FRED-I-BEAR". Fred being my grandfather's name and the name of a very special friend.

The number of teddy bear collectors in South Africa is very small, so I needed to exhibit at countries where there was a greater demand. I attended my first teddy bear exhibition in the Untied Kingdom about three years ago. I have since exhibited in Germany, Switzerland and Vienna, and I am hoping to now exhibit in Japan. I have won first and second places in Vienna and I am a 2002 nominee in the TTTA competition.

I have learned to make bears through trial and error, but I completed a one-day workshop with Gregory Gyllenship and learned a few more bear-making tricks from him. The most important thing for me in my bear making is to enjoy it. If you love what you are doing, it will show in the finished product even if the ears, eyes or nose are not always perfect. I make my bears heavy by adding glass beads and try and get them come to life by adding shiny noses and painted features for added depth. I can always be found in a teddy bear shop or looking at teddy bear magazines on my travels. I find that it is always a source of inspiration, and I then cannot wait to get back home to try out new designs. I'm the same way with new fabric. It seems to speak to me.

I never had a teddy bear as a child, but I love all animals, which is where I get my love for bears. Just as I speak to and love my dogs, I also speak to and love my bears. Bears that look sad and floppy will always find a place in my own collection. Teddy bears seem to reach out to people and you can never be too young or old to love a teddy bear. I have seen the pleasure that they bring to both young and old. Seeing a collector's eye sparkle when they take home a bear of mine makes me happy.

I would like to tell all teddy bear makers never to give up. If your bear is not perfect, he is still special as you made him. And to all the collectors out there in the world, thank-you. Without you I would never be able to share my love of bears.

Contact Details

Lynette Kennedy
Fred-I-Bear
P O Box 6502
Westgate, 1734
South Africa

Tel: +27-11-672-4008
Fax: +27-11-672-4008
Email: lck@mweb.co.za
Website: www.fred-i-bear.co.za

Materials Needed

a fat ¼ yard/meter mohair
4in x 4in (10cm x 10cm) square of wool felt for paw and foot pads
one pair of 9mm or 10mm black glass eyes
ten 30mm discs for joints
ten cotter pin or lock nut sets
DMC No.8 black Perle embroidery cotton for nose and mouth
airbrush equipment or fabric marker pens for face shading
small strand of faux pearls for the necklace
Silk roses and an old piece of decorative lace for the shawl
general sewing notions and bear making tools

Special Instructions

First trace off all pattern pieces onto a firm plastic sheet or strong cardboard making sure that all markings are transferred onto the templates. Remember to reverse necessary pieces when cutting out mohair.

Cut all pattern pieces following nap direction and reversing as necessary. Mark openings and joint positions.

Join head and side pieces sewing from A to B. Sew gusset from A to C. Tack gusset first to prevent it from slipping as you work.

Join leg pieces together leaving an opening for stuffing. Attach paw pad to foot opening.

Attach paw pad to inner arm, and join arm pieces leaving an opening for stuffing.

Join two back pieces together and two front pieces together. Join back to front. Leave opening for stuffing.

Start filling head by firmly filling in snout area and working towards the opening. Snout must be firm as it is easier to embroider the nose. At opening of neck, place a disk and pin. With very strong thread, gather up around the neck edge around the joint.

Mark positions of eyes. Turn bear upside down or look at it in a mirror to check that the eyes are even. Attach eyes with a strong thread.

Attach head to body making sure that you tighten the cotter pin (nut and bolt) securely.

Stuff arms and legs ¾ of the way and attach to body. When attached and firm, finish and close off openings with a ladder stitch.

Stuff tummy, closing the opening using a ladder stitch. Small glass beads can be added to the tummy to make the bear heavier.

Mark nose with a water-soluble pen, and embroider mouth.

Join ear pieces and attach to head with a ladder stitch. Again, if you turn the bear upside down you will get a better feel for the ear positions.

Tips

Allow a ¼in or 5mm seam allowance when sewing pieces together.

Check that all body pieces have been sewn on both sides before turning it the right way. Also brush out on the wrong side any pieces of mohair that might have gotten caught up in the stitching. This will give you a much better seam.

When making a label/card for your bear always include on it what you have used to make the bear, and whether it is a limited edition.

To add more character to your bear you can always use crayon to smudge around the nose and eye area.

Tighten the screws or cotter pins as firmly as possible but still allowing movement, as trapped mohair between the body pieces will flatten with time and make them looser.

Make all joint markings on the fabric.

Use Fray-Check™ if the fabric you are working with tends to fray.

Remember, just as we are human beings with our own special quirks, so your bear has its own unique character. That's what makes them so special. Relax and enjoy your bear making.

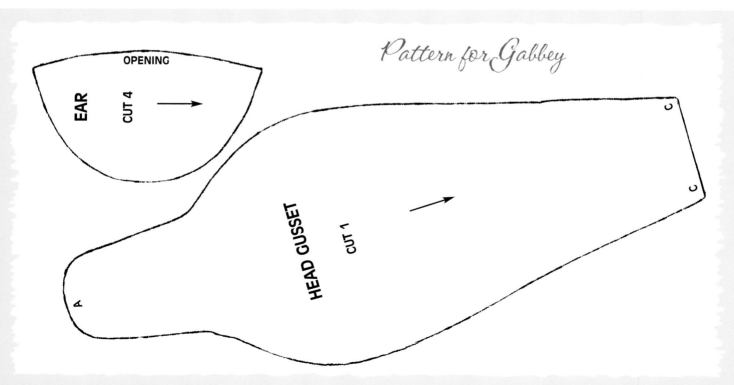

Pattern for Gabbey

EAR
CUT 4
OPENING

HEAD GUSSET
CUT 1

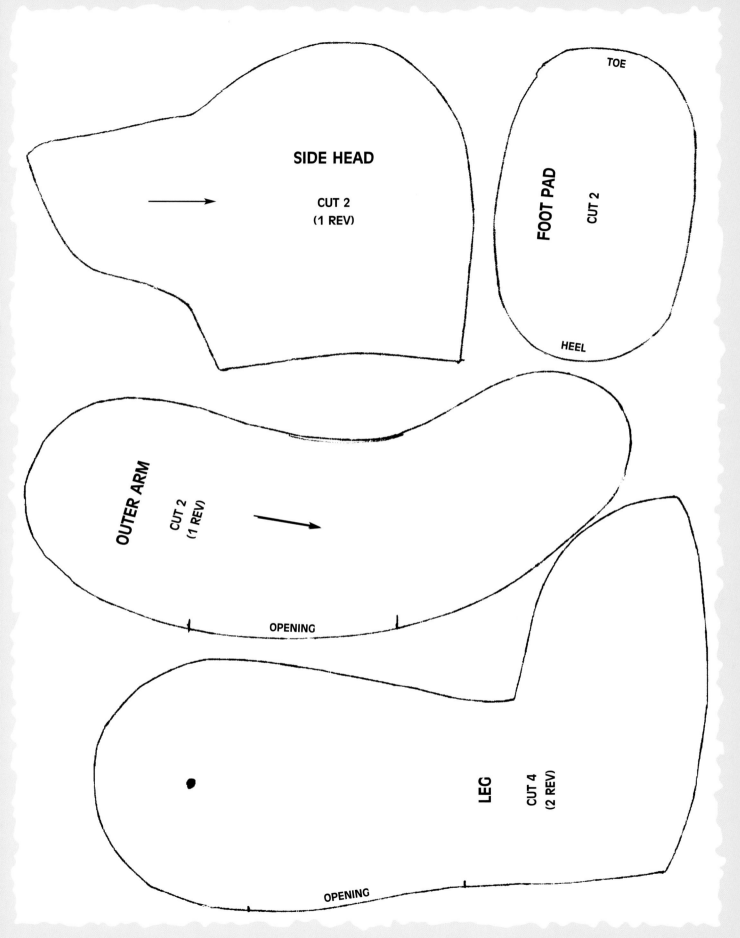

SIDE HEAD

CUT 2
(1 REV)

TOE

FOOT PAD

CUT 2

HEEL

OUTER ARM

CUT 2
(1 REV)

OPENING

LEG

CUT 4
(2 REV)

OPENING

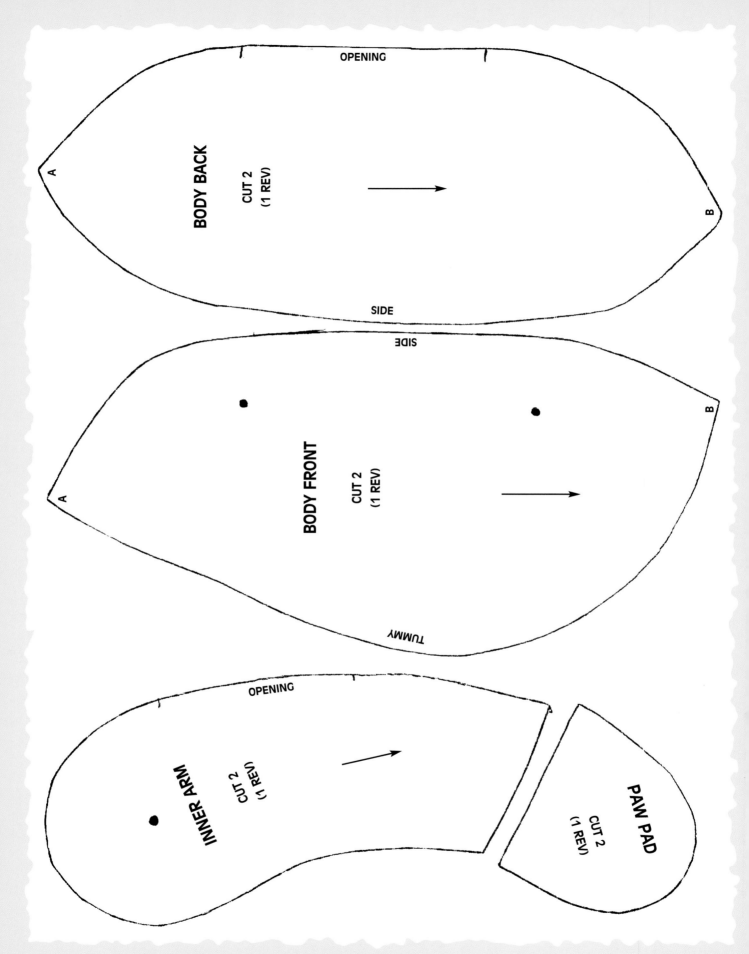

OPENING

BODY BACK

CUT 2
(1 REV)

A

B

SIDE

SIDE

B

BODY FRONT

CUT 2
(1 REV)

A

TUMMY

OPENING

INNER ARM

CUT 2
(1 REV)

PAW PAD

CUT 2
(1 REV)

Seymour
15in (38cm). Contemporary bear.

Marietjie Coertzen–Marieque Bears

Marietjie Coertzen is the owner and producer of Marieque Bears. Marietjie's sewing skills started when her grandmother taught her how to crochet at the age of five. That early start lead to sewing for herself and her three daughters. She also excelled at many needlework crafts. Quilting was a passion that lasted for more than 12 years and she won many national and international prizes with her beautiful quilts.

Quite by chance, a friend invited her to a teddy bear show and, intrigued, she went. That was the moment of decision. She was so enamored with the skills and care displayed in the making of the teddy bears that she decided to also make a teddy or two. Marietjie attended teddy bear making classes, and after a few months of experimentation, she developed her own "brand" of handcrafted bears. Each Marieque teddy bear is meticulously made and careful attention is given to every detail. Each bear has its own uniquely appealing face that seems to be irresistible to his or her new owners. At her very first teddy bear show, she won first prize. Marieque Bears have also been featured in local craft magazines.

Today, just five years later, her teddy bears are eagerly sought after and have become collector's items. Marieque Bears are sold to exclusive teddy bear boutiques and a stream of loyal private customers. Due to the demand for Marieque Bears, and the fact that she works alone, her teddy bears customers are quite often placed on a waiting list.

For the past two years, Marietjie has been teaching the art of teddy bear making. The delight on the faces of new collectors when they view their creations for the first time is very gratifying.

Contact Details

Marietjie Coertzen
Marieque Bears
35 Monkor Road
Randpark Ridge
Randburg, 2194
South Africa

Tel: +27-11-478-3601/678-7032
Fax: +27-11-678-7032
Email: coertzen@mweb.co.za

Materials Needed

a fat ¼ yard/meter mohair
8in x 8in (20cm x 20cm) square of ultra suede for paw and foot pads
one pair of 10mm black glass eyes
ten 50mm discs for joints
ten cotter pin or lock nut sets
DMC No.5 black Perle embroidery cotton for nose and mouth
general sewing notions and bear making tools

Special Instructions:

Seymour is a very easy pattern. Please refer to the general bear making instructions covered in the book.

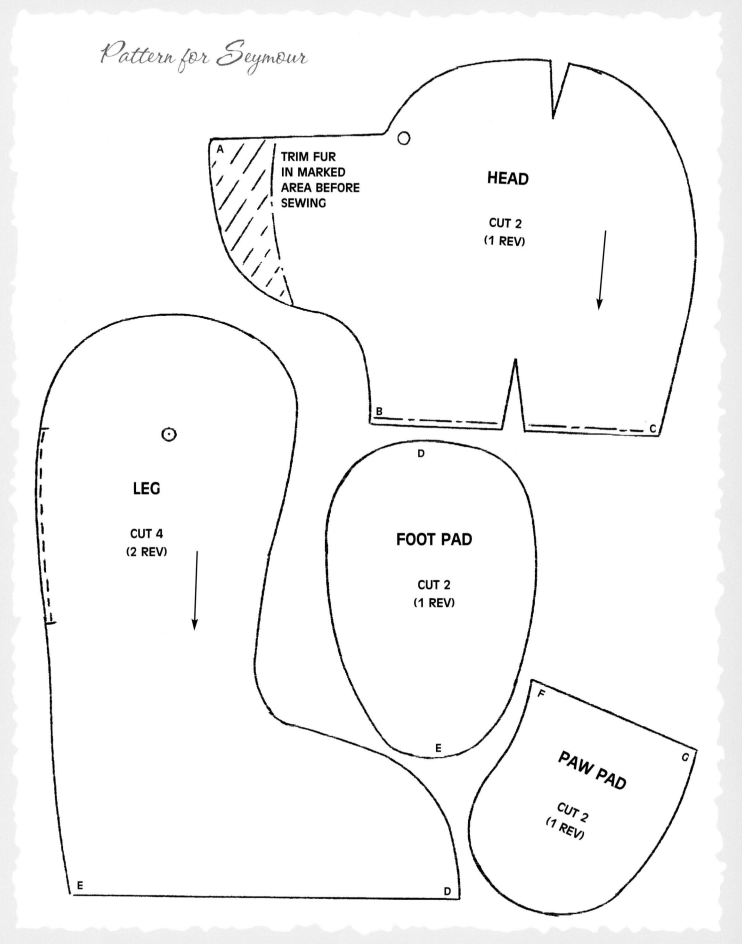

Pattern for Seymour

**TRIM FUR
IN MARKED
AREA BEFORE
SEWING**

A

HEAD

**CUT 2
(1 REV)**

B

C

LEG

**CUT 4
(2 REV)**

FOOT PAD

**CUT 2
(1 REV)**

D

E

E

D

F

PAW PAD

**CUT 2
(1 REV)**

G

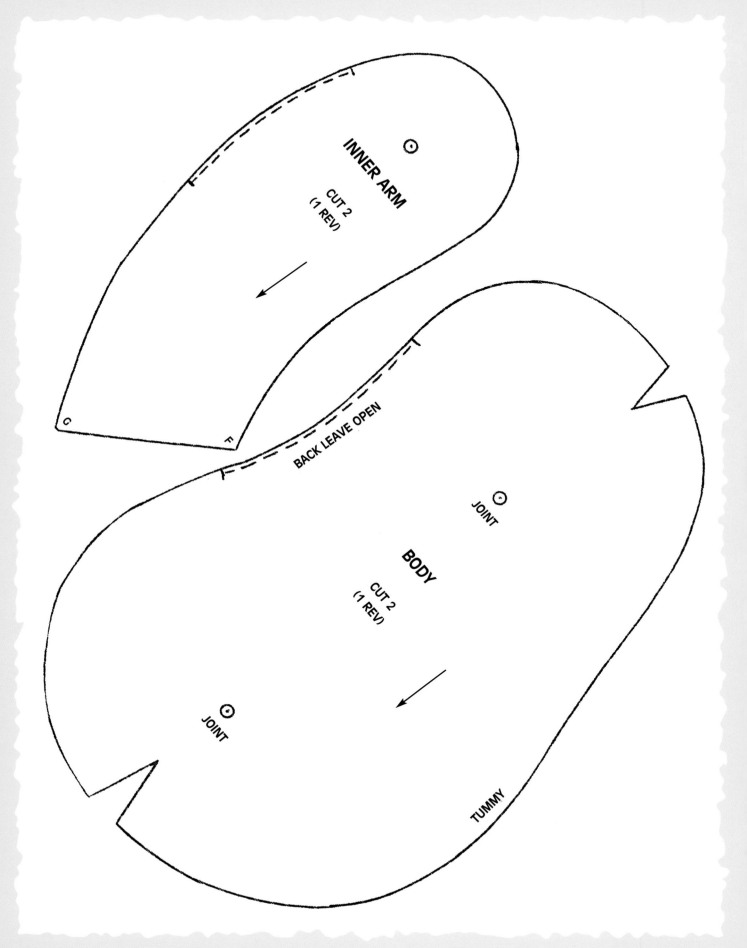

INNER ARM

CUT 2
(1 REV)

C

F

BACK LEAVE OPEN

JOINT

BODY

CUT 2
(1 REV)

JOINT

TUMMY

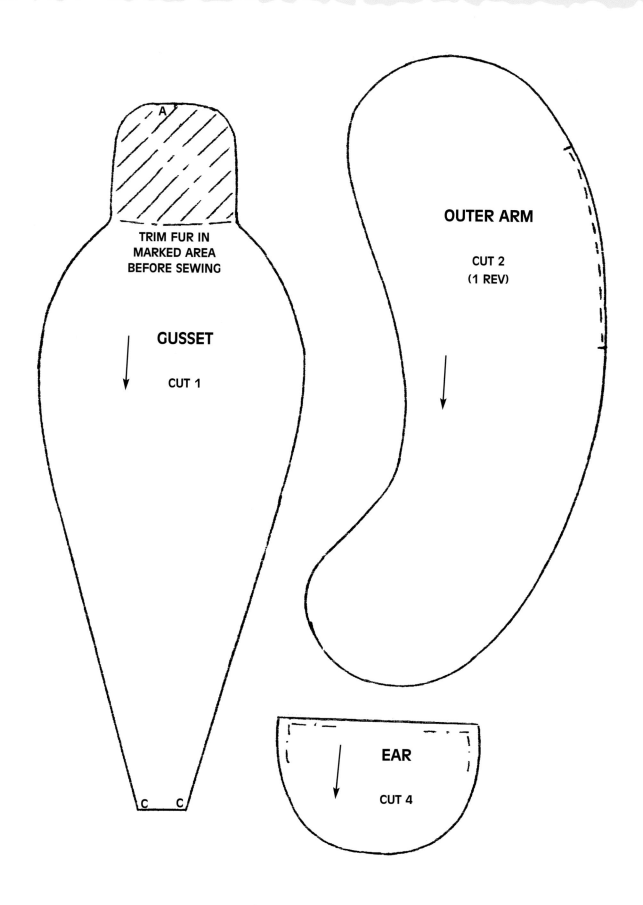

A

TRIM FUR IN
MARKED AREA
BEFORE SEWING

GUSSET

↓

CUT 1

C   C

OUTER ARM

CUT 2
(1 REV)

↓

EAR

↓

CUT 4

Spike
12in (31cm). Bear with airbrush detail.

Jackie Mitchell–Sinclair Bears

I have always had an interest in art and sewing. I started making bears in the early 1980's, but of course they were made out of synthetic material. My husband, Rob, bought my first ¼m piece of German Mohair in Durban in 1996. It made the most beautiful bear. I was hooked. I have won a couple of local awards. Airbrushing makes the bears come alive. It's the part I love the most as it gives me such personal satisfaction. Enjoy making your bear!

Contact Details

Jackie Mitchell
Sinclair Bears
Eversdal, 7550
Durbanville
South Africa

Tel: + 27-21- 919-6183
Email: Jackiemit@hotmail.com

Materials Needed
17½in x 23½in (45cm x 60cm) mohair
9in x 4in (23cm x 10cm) ultra suede
one pair 7mm glass eyes
DMC No. 5 black perle cotton for nose
strong thread for eyes
polyester filling
plastic pellets for filling stomach
excelsior or wood wool for stuffing nose
40mm locknut joint set for arms and head
50mm locknut joint set for legs

Special Instructions
Once the head is stuffed, and the ears, nose and neck joint are in place, the eyes can be put on.

Eyes
Extra strong thread must be used. A doll needle must be dusted with talcum powder. Make a hole with a long thread form A through to B. Knot first eye onto long double thread. Insert needle at point A. Thread needle through first eye shank. The thread must be pulled very tightly sinking the eyes.

Reinsert your needle as close to point A eye as possible, coming out at the bottom of the head.

Stuffing
Excelsior or wood wool is packed firmly into the nose of the bear. Polyester filling is used in the arms, legs and the rest of the head. Pellets with small loose balls of polyester filling can be used in the body to make a soft huggable bear.

Airbrushing
Airbrushing or special pens can bring your bear to life. Study the markings on real bears to get the most natural effect..

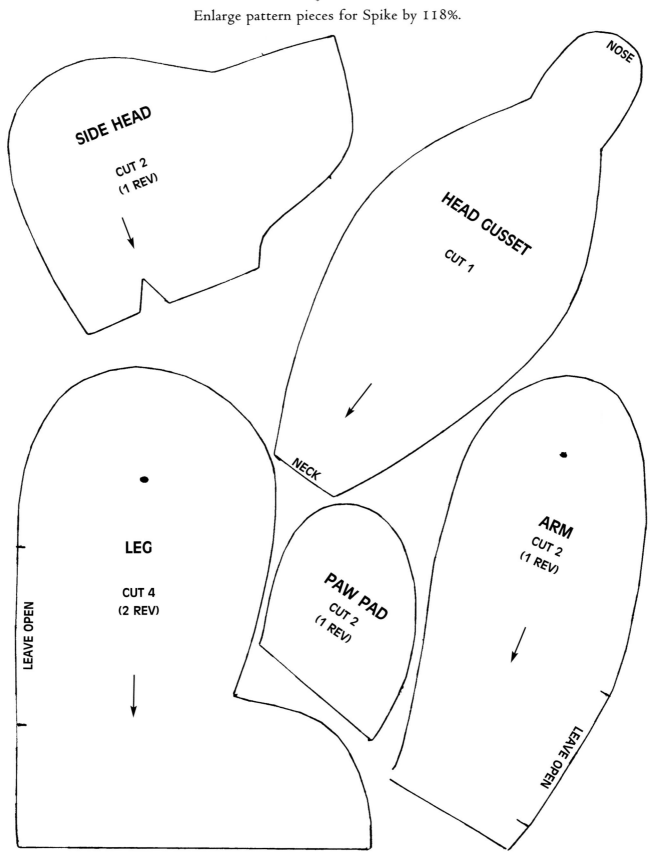

Enlarge pattern pieces for Spike by 118%.

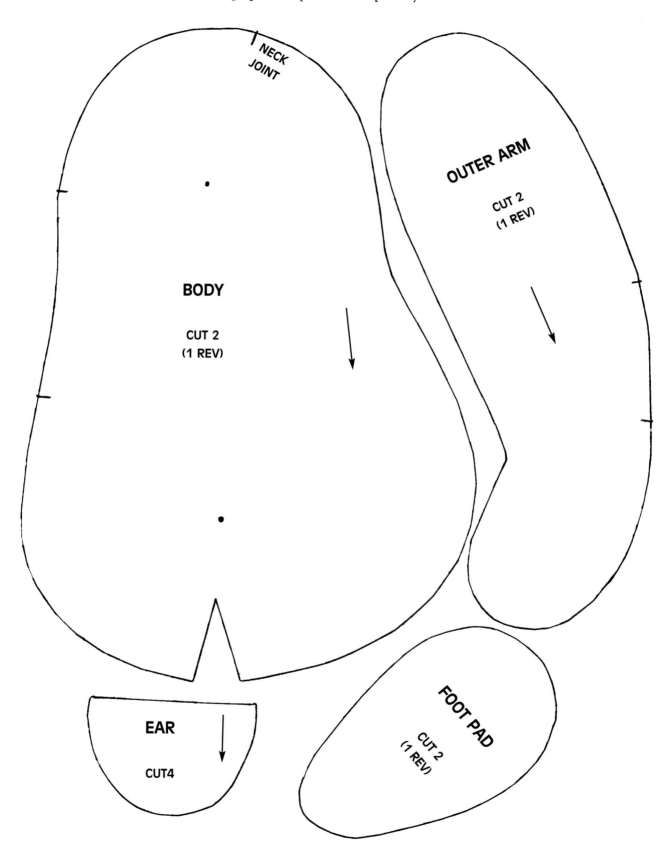

Jeannette

14in (36cm). Bear with bent arms and legs.

The Artist
Lynne Thomson–Bearlyn Bears

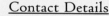

I started bear making after buying a kit and making it up. That was eight years ago. Mohair wasn't as readily available back then so most of my first bears were made with synthetic fabric. After the completion of my first bear, Monty, I was hooked. I started making bears from commercial patterns and slowly started to do my own designs. I use my own designs exclusively now. My bears are made with a lot of love and, more importantly, a great deal of attention. My sizes vary from about 2½in to 20in (6cm-51cm). Most of them are one of a kind or part of very small limited edition.

My favorites are the big bears - 12in (31cm) and up. I only use the best mohair. I love the tipped mohair, which is mainly Schulte. For the paw pads, I use ultra suede, wool felt and sometime reverse the fabric when needed. For the smaller bears, I joint them with cotter pins, but I use the Nyloc™ nuts and screws for the larger ones. I fill my bears with polyester filling and glass beads or plastic pellets. My favorite bears are the traditional bears, but sometimes I do something a bit different. I use glass eyes and all my bears' noses are hand-embroidered.

Contact Details

Lynne Thomson
Bearlyn Bears
PO Box 76
Sarnia, 3615
South Africa

Tel/Fax: +27-31-708-1159
Cell: +27-82-870-5349
Email: thommies@iafica.com

Materials Needed

This bear can be stitched by machine if preferred.

- ½ yard/meter mohair
- ultra suede
- 10mm eyes
- ten 45cm discs
- one 4mm screw for neck
- one nut for neck screw
- four 2mm screws for arms and legs
- four Nyloc™ nuts
- ten washers
- nose thread
- polyester filling
- thread to stitch
- sharp pointed embroidery scissors
- pliers and screwdriver for nuts
- pen to mark out pattern
- pins
- awl
- long needle
- needle with which to stitch

Preparation

Needle in machine No. 80
Stitch on No. 2 stitch
A ¼in or 5mm seam allowance is allowed in the pattern. Use your discretion as to whether it will be strong enough.
Read instructions carefully

Special Instructions

Please refer to the general bear making instructions covered in the book.

Tips

When you insert the neck screw, washer and disc into the head, pull thread tight until only the pin can been seen. Over stitch the folds around the cotter pin so they lie flat. This will strengthen your neck joint and ensure less wear.

If you are sewing by machine, sew twice to reinforce your seams for extra strength.

Pattern for Jeannette

Enlarge pattern pieces for Jeannette by 135%.

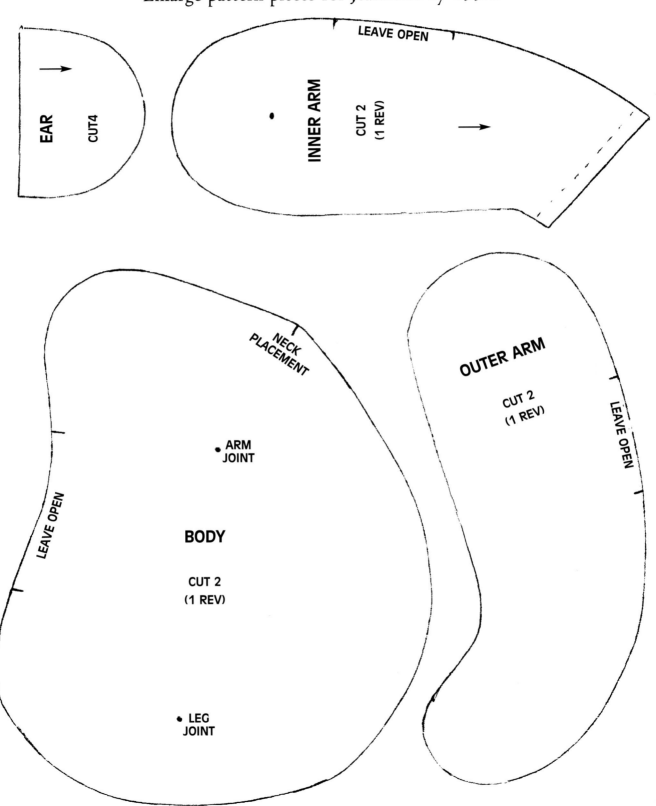

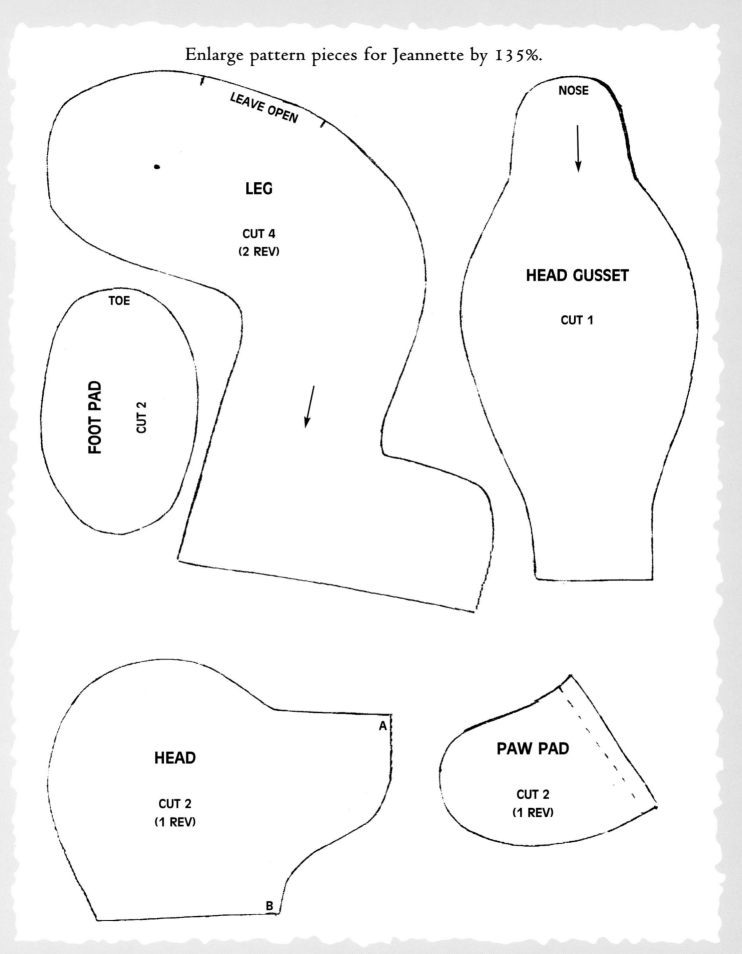

Enlarge pattern pieces for Jeannette by 135%.

LEAVE OPEN

LEG

CUT 4
(2 REV)

NOSE

HEAD GUSSET

CUT 1

TOE

FOOT PAD

CUT 2

HEAD

CUT 2
(1 REV)

A

B

PAW PAD

CUT 2
(1 REV)

Richard
16in (41cm). Traditional bear.

The Artist

Eunice Beaton–Teddytech

I have been active in making teddy bears as a craft and art form since 1982 and have thus become the doyenne of South African teddy bear making. Unable to find suitable mohair for teddy bears during that time, I collaborated with a textile technologist at the CSIR (Council for Scientific and Industrial Research) in South Africa that then produced mohair specifically for teddy bears and I promoted it both locally and internationally.

My passion for bear making led me to designing kits for the local market in 1992 and after numerous requests, I started teaching, thus unraveling the mystery of bear making! In 1994, I opened my specialist bear shop, *Thread Bears*, the first of its kind in Durban and it has become a "must visit" on the itinerary of all prospective and converted bear makers!

I enjoy creating both traditional and contemporary styled bears and have exhibited at various fairs in England, at Linda Mullins' show in San Diego, USA and Teddybar Total in Hennef, Germany.

Contact Details
Tel: +27 31 312 7755
Fax: +27 31 312 9564
Email: ebeaton@global.co.za

Materials Needed
¼ yard/meter mohair, includes sufficient to reverse fabric for paws and footpads
ten 50mm wooden discs
one cotter pin, two washers – for head
four lock nuts, four bolts, eight washers – arms and legs
one pair 10mm or 11mm glass eyes
black or brown embroidery thread – nose, mouth, claws
fine needle if hand-stitching
darner needle
sewing thread in color to match fabric
polyester filling
spanner and screwdriver
long-nosed pliers
optional: bear maker's floss

Special Instructions
Please refer to the general bear making instructions covered in the book.

Enlarge pattern pieces for Richard by 170%.

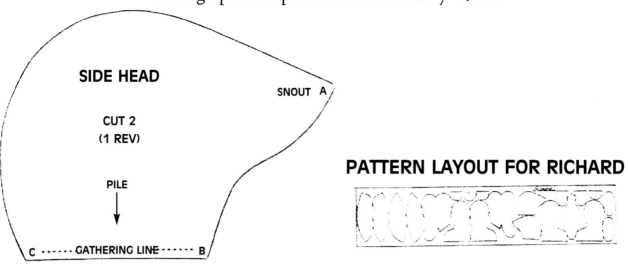

SIDE HEAD

CUT 2
(1 REV)

SNOUT A

PILE

C ·····GATHERING LINE····· B

PATTERN LAYOUT FOR RICHARD

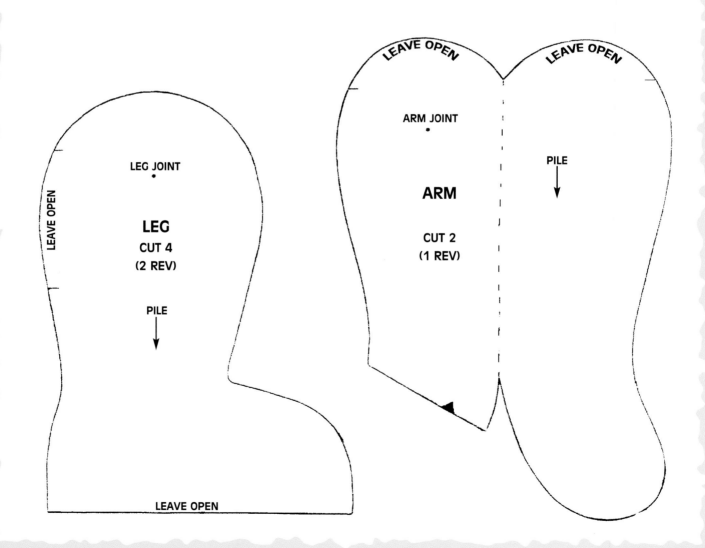

LEAVE OPEN

LEAVE OPEN

ARM JOINT

ARM

CUT 2
(1 REV)

PILE

LEG JOINT

LEAVE OPEN

LEG
CUT 4
(2 REV)

PILE

LEAVE OPEN

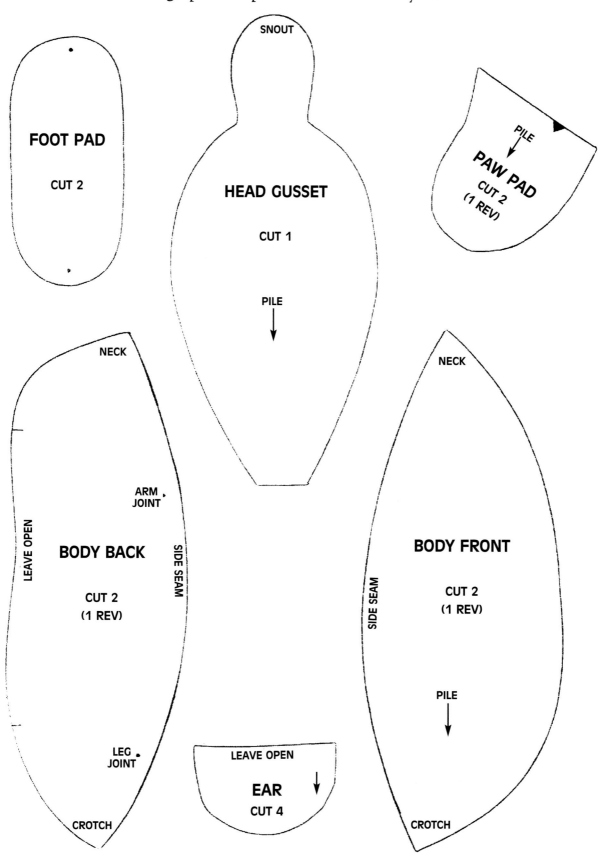

Lizz-Bee
16in (41cm). Bee bear with wings and antennae.

The Artist
Michela Rae—raeBear Collectibles

I have always been an avid bear collector and only discovered in late 1999 that I could make one of my own. I had walked into a local newsagent and found a step-by-step book to make teddy bears and thought what the heck? It took me a while to find stockists of bear supplies, but when I did, nothing could stop me. Funnily enough, I'm more obsessed than ever with collecting bears perhaps because I appreciate them more now. Another obsession I've developed is collecting vast amounts of mohair just in case I might need that particular color for something.

I started designing my own patterns soon after I began making bears and then entered a local annual bear competition in 2000 and won first place for a 16in (41cm) bear called Maple. Now I'm hooked and have no intention of doing anything else. Lizz-Bee is one of my favorites and I hope you enjoy making her.

Contact Details

Michela Rae
Postal: PO Box 418
Plettenberg Bay, 6600
South Africa

Tel: +2744-531-6608
Fax: +2744-531-6674
Email: raebearza@global.co.za
Website: www.raebears.homestead.com

Materials Needed
fat ¼ yard/meter of gold wavy mohair
¹/16 yard/meter of black wavy mohair
fat ¼ yard/meter of white tulle fabric for wings
ten 50mm discs and washers
seven cotter pins
three imitation silk sunflowers
one pair 10mm glass eyes
No. 5 DMC perle cotton for nose
one black chenille pipe cleaner for antennae
matching ultra suede for paw pads
black marker or airbrush for shading
long thick needle to thread the antennae

Special Instructions
Please refer to the general bear making instructions covered in the book to make up the head, arms and legs. It is very important to take note of the color requirements for the different body pieces. Also remember that the ears must be black. Trim the muzzle and side head pieces before sewing.

Body

The pieces are marked 1 through 5— 1 is the top part and 5 is the bottom. Cut the pieces according to the colors required and remember the pile direction. Pin no. 1 to no. 2 and then sew in place. Then pin No. 2 to No. 3 and sew in place. Continue this for both sides of the body until all pieces are joined and coordinated from the top—black/gold/black/gold/black.

Wobble Jointing For The Legs

For Lizz-Bee I used wobble joints in the legs for posability and a regular joint for the neck and arms. To make up the wobble joints, splay the ends of one cotter pin and slip one of the ends into the loop of another cotter pin so that they are joined through their loops. Insert a disc over one of the cotter pins with a washer and secure by turning with a cotter pin turner or pliers. Then insert as normal ensuring that they are secured very tightly. This method allows for a "relaxed" sitting pose for a bear with bent legs.

Wings

Cut 4 sets of wings on the fold from the tulle fabric. **This piece is the actual size so there is no need to enlarge it.** Place all pieces together and pin at the center. Using a running stitch, gather the layers together and secure in place at the center point. Take one of the silk sunflowers and sew it to the center point. Find a spot just under the hump on Lizz-Bee's back and sew in place with a few stitches. If you would like to add a special feature to the wings, use some glitter glue around the edges and the folds.

Antennae

Use Lizz-Bee's photograph as a guide for this procedure. When her head is stuffed and after the ears have been attached, find a point at the top front of the ear and mark it with a black marker. Then find the matching point in front of the other ear. Using a very thick needle, thread the chenille pipe cleaner from one point and out the other. Ensure that the visible pieces are of equal lengths. Stitch these in place at the exit points to secure. Now, with the remaining sunflowers, stitch these in place as per Lizz-Bee's photograph. Then curl the pipe cleaners forward with your fingers until they match.

Shading

Using an airbrush or black marker, shade the eye area before the eyes are set. Shade the muzzle in a triangular shape before sewing the nose and mouth. When the nose and mouth are complete, shade the area in the center if the mouth in a circular motion.

Nose

Use bees wax rubbing up and down in the direction of the stitches. With some brown paper buff the nose every now and then in a circular motion. Continue doing this until the nose surface is smooth and it is difficult to see the individual stitches.

LEAVE OPEN

LEG
CUT 4
(2 REV)

ARM
CUT 2
(1 REV)

LEAVE OPEN

PAW PAD
CUT 2
(1 REV)

FOOT PAD
CUT 2
(1 REV)

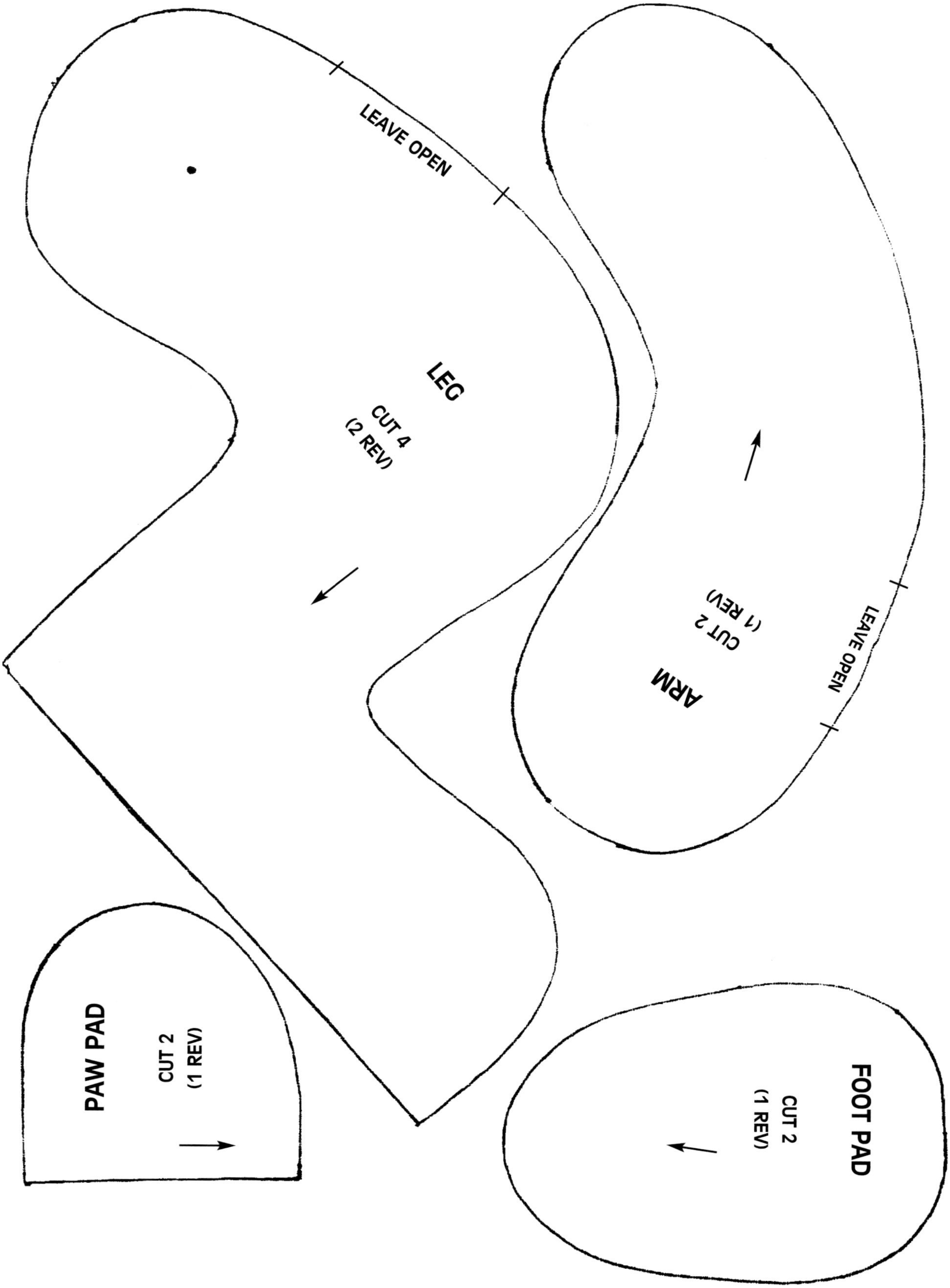

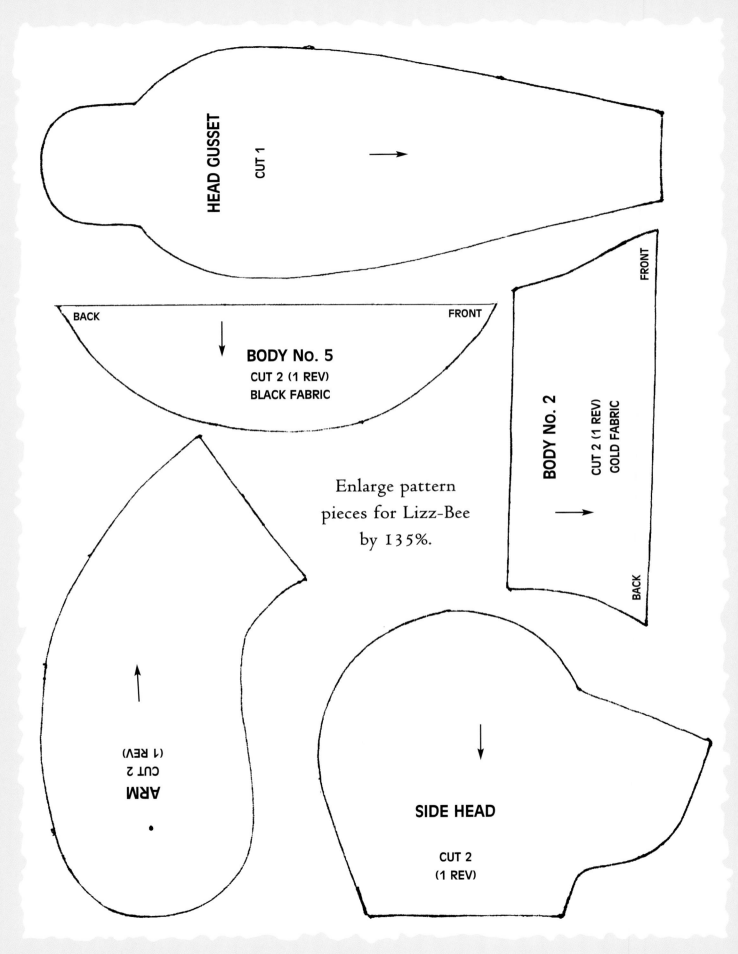

HEAD GUSSET

CUT 1

BODY No. 5

CUT 2 (1 REV)

BLACK FABRIC

BACK

FRONT

BODY No. 2

CUT 2 (1 REV)
GOLD FABRIC

FRONT

BACK

Enlarge pattern
pieces for Lizz-Bee
by 135%.

ARM
CUT 2
(1 REV)

SIDE HEAD

CUT 2
(1 REV)

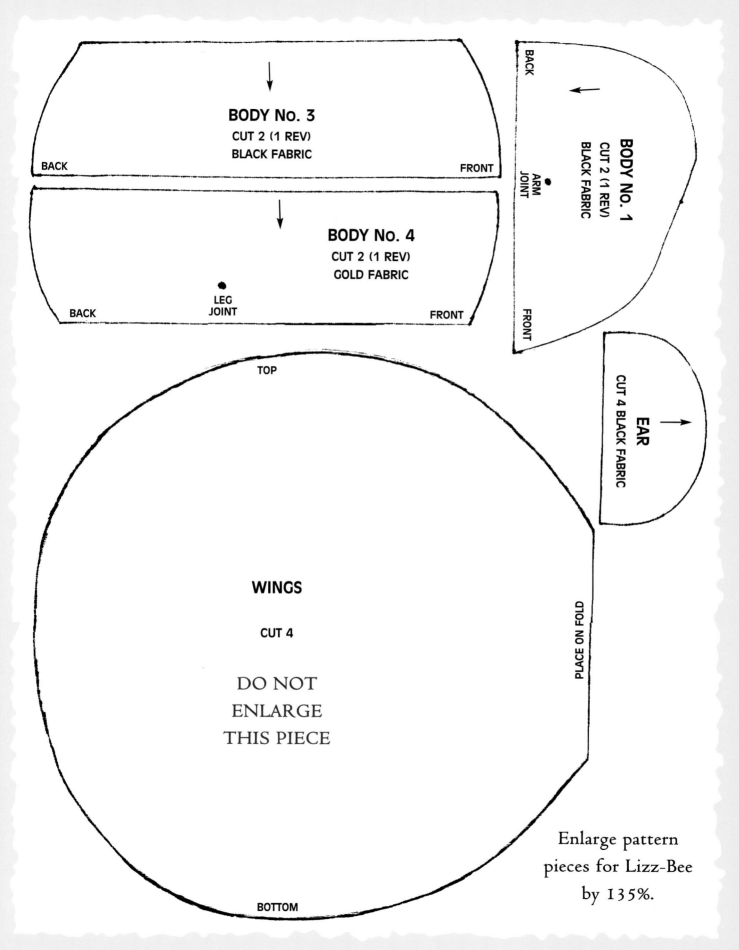

BODY No. 3
CUT 2 (1 REV)
BLACK FABRIC

BACK

FRONT

BODY No. 4
CUT 2 (1 REV)
GOLD FABRIC

BACK

LEG
JOINT

FRONT

BODY No. 1
CUT 2 (1 REV)
BLACK FABRIC

BACK

ARM
JOINT

FRONT

EAR
CUT 4 BLACK FABRIC

TOP

WINGS

CUT 4

DO NOT
ENLARGE
THIS PIECE

PLACE ON FOLD

Enlarge pattern
pieces for Lizz-Bee
by 135%.

BOTTOM

Codswallop
18in (46cm). Character bear.

The Artist
Nerina Roberts—Honeydew Bears

I suppose my bear making really began in the 1970's when I found myself housebound with 2 young children. I began making soft toys, including the occasional bear, using patterns found in magazines. I found some giraffe print fur fabric, which was quite notable back then, as fur fabrics were scarce. I was unable to find a suitable pattern for the fabric so I opted to design one instead with the aid of my draftsman husband.

Inspired by this experience, I learned to design cloth dolls and toys and soon moved on to soft sculpture cloth dolls, winning many awards in the process of perfecting my techniques. I had 2 books published on the subject.

In the early 1990's, I attended a bear show in England and was immediately keen to try my hand at bears. I arrived back home with a good supply of books, mohair and all kinds of bear-making supplies to get started. Since then, I have been making and designing bears with a preference for unusual characters.

Today, I run a large bear-making supply store with my husband Fred and daughter Anne-Marie where we supply imported mohair and bear-making requirements. We also run workshops every weekend hosted by other well-known artists and ourselves.

Contact Details

Nerina Roberts
Honeydew Bears
PO Box 73422
Fairland, 2030
South Africa

Tel: +27-11-678-5834
Fax: +27-11-678-5834
Email: honeydewbears@vwol.co.za

Materials Needed

fat ¼ yard/meter mohair
suede for paw pads
one pair of 14mm glass teddy bear eyes
one set teddy joints - six 40mm, four 35mm
polyester filling
plastic pellets
embroidery thread for nose
usual sewing supplies

Special Instructions

This "bear" really is just a bit of Codswallop. Great new shape! Big feet, big hands, extra fat tummy and a long snout. Great news is that I have given you two head patterns. "A" has a long snout if you feel up to embroidering an elaborate nose. "B" is a new design where you can embroider a big triangular nose simply by following the outline of the gusset.

Once you've decided on the head of your choice, please refer to the general bear making instructions covered in the book.

Pattern for Codswallop

Enlarge pattern pieces for Codswallop by 170%.

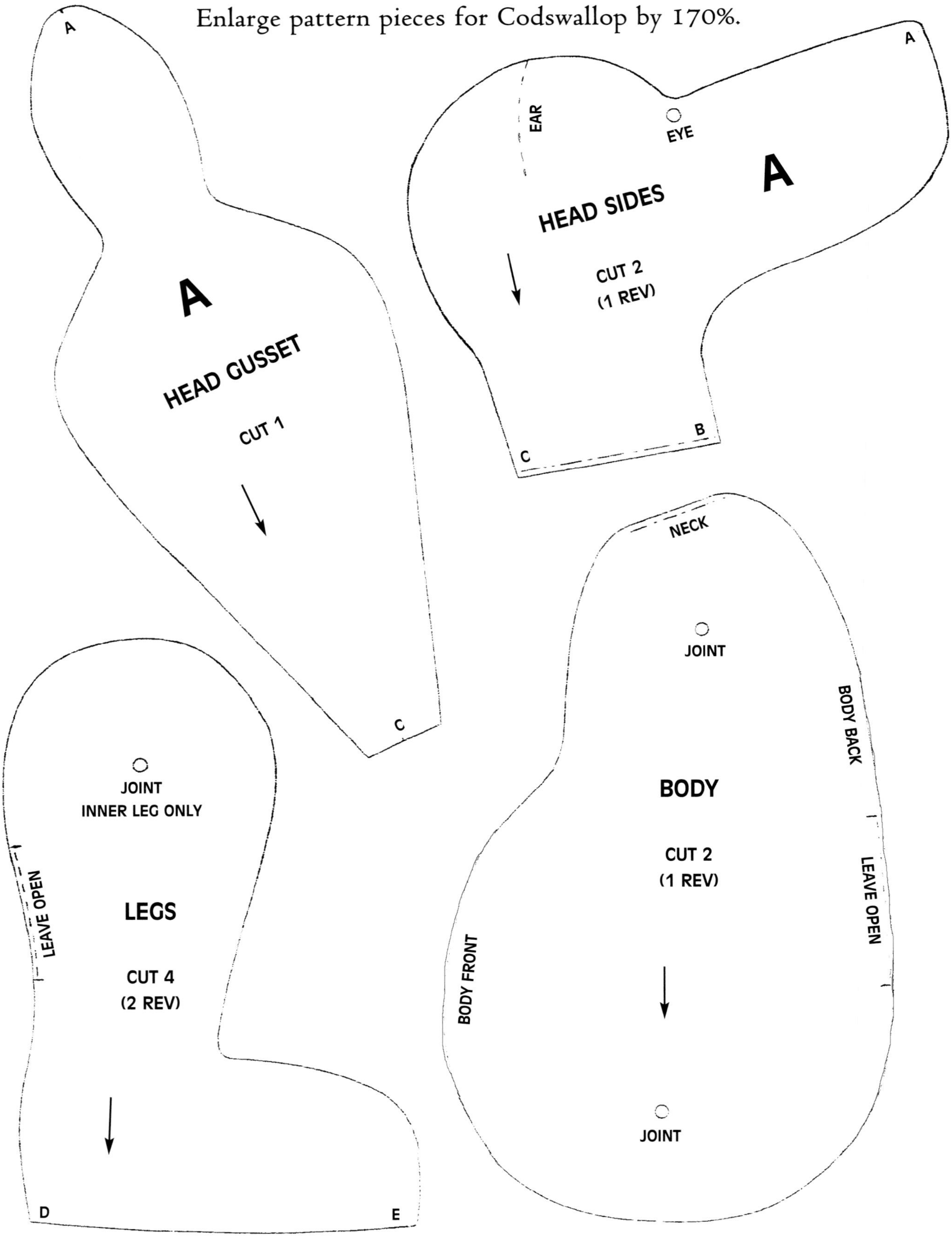

A

HEAD GUSSET

CUT 1

EAR

EYE

HEAD SIDES

A

CUT 2
(1 REV)

C

B

NECK

JOINT

BODY BACK

BODY

CUT 2
(1 REV)

BODY FRONT

LEAVE OPEN

JOINT

C

JOINT
INNER LEG ONLY

LEAVE OPEN

LEGS

CUT 4
(2 REV)

D

E

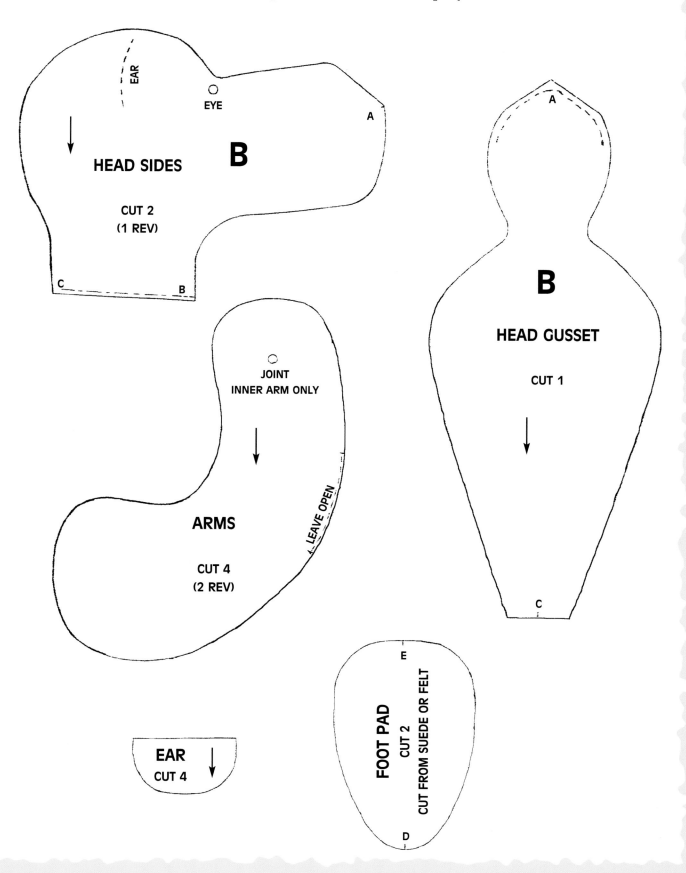

Big Brother
24in (61cm). Fully-jointed bear with bent arms.

The Artist

Kit Mills–EastCape Bears

Kit Mills saw a lovely bear in a department store in a little farming town in South Africa when she was seven. She used to visit the shop on her own and look at the bear and hold its hand. She was surprised and delighted to receive it for her eighth birthday in 1938, and still has a photograph taken on that day. Four years later, she made her first teddy bear using woolen fabric.

When traveling in England in 1990, she was intrigued to see bears being made and sold by Shirley Latimer in a small shop in Alcester. This really fired her imagination and resulted in a joyous hobby. She has to "feel a bear coming on" before she makes one. They are all different. Large huggable bears are her favorites. She derives special pleasure from using the best materials available, like German mohair and growlers, Austrian crystal glass eyes, Swiss musical boxes, and fine South African leather for the pads. Many of the bears are totally hand sewn just for the pleasure of it, and because they tend to feel softer.

She attends only one bear festival annually in Cape Town. She received the First Prize for Large Bears (over 18 inches) at the Buitenverwagting Bear Fair in beautiful Constantia, Cape Town in 1996 and again in 1999. Kit enters her bears and other animals in the handcraft section of the local Bathurst Agricultural Show and has won several First Prizes including "Best Article in Handcrafts" twice. Four of her bears appear in Marc Hobermann's *Teddy Bear Book*. Many now reside in the USA, Scotland, England, Germany, Austria, Australia and Singapore as well as in South Africa. Each bear has something about his nature written on its neck tag. Big Brother's label states that he has an adventurous nature and would like to take up acting as his main hobby.

Contact Details

Kit Mills
EastCape Bears
PO Box 577
Grahamstown, 6140
South Africa

Tel: +27-46-622-9719
Email: kitmills@foyn.co.za

Materials Needed

1 yard/meter mohair
one pair 15mm or 16mm glass eyes
large square of leather or ultra suede
six 3in (8cm) discs for neck and legs
four 2½in (6cm) discs for arms
five large bolts and nuts
ten washers
one growler
brown perle cotton for nose and claws

Big Brother is a very challenging pattern and should only be attempted once you have confidently gained some experience and patience.

Special Instructions

The discs used in the neck and legs are three inches in diameter, and those in the arms are two and a half inches in diameter. The eyes are backed with cream leather discs cut the same size as the eyes at $1/16$ in, but with an off center hole punched in them so that they hang below the eyes to give the face more expression. It is best to glue the leather to the eye, and then to glue the underside of the leather to the fur fabric of the face.

When the eyes have been inserted and the string hangs out the back of the head, tie the strings of each eye together so you can insert your finger through the loop, then pull the loop while pressing the eye with your thumb. Doing both eyes at the same time allows for better judgment in the placing of the eyes.

If the eyes are not glued in, it is a good idea to leave the strings tied and hanging out for a day or two in case you decide to move one or both eyes. The hands are made separately from the arms, and then inserted, matching the symbols given (the seams do not coincide.) This is so that the hands will look more realistic.

The easiest way to attach the sewn hand to the arm is to leave an opening below the elbow that goes to within one and a half inches of the wrist. With wrong side of arm outwards, insert the point of the hand (with fur side out) into the wrist hole, and sew, matching the symbols. Turn the arm right side out; insert the disc and stuff in the usual way.

For a big bear like Big Brother, it would be better to use bolts and self-locking nuts than cotter pins. This would stop him from getting arthritis in his old age. If Big Brother is ever to fulfill his dreams of becoming an actor he is going to need a large growler.

Put the growler inside a piece of cut off stocking, and tie it in with the knots at the sides of the growler.

For a nice firm nose, draw the outline with big stitches and sew the inside horizontally, then vertically.

ONE MORE TIP: I think it is a good idea to line the pads if they are made of felt or some other material that will wear through. Remember that bears can "live" as long as people do, sometimes longer. Just imagine how an old bear feels with exfoliating dermatitis on his palms and soles! Sew claws on Big Brother's hands and feet if desired. If the fur is so thick that the claws do not show on Big Brother, take some strong thread the same color as the pads, and put in four long claw-type stitches on the sole instead, pulling them tight, and then join the stitches at the bottom.

The shape of the pads on the feet does not lend itself to this treatment. I asked Big Brother if he would like different shaped footpads and he said not to bother as he seldom walks on his hands. (I think he is confused!)

Fold the foot pads in half to find the center point at the heel. Pin this to the heel seam on the leg and maneuver the fabric around the pad until it fits comfortably. You should have a right and left foot.

Pattern for Big Brother

Enlarge pattern pieces for Big Brother by 170%.

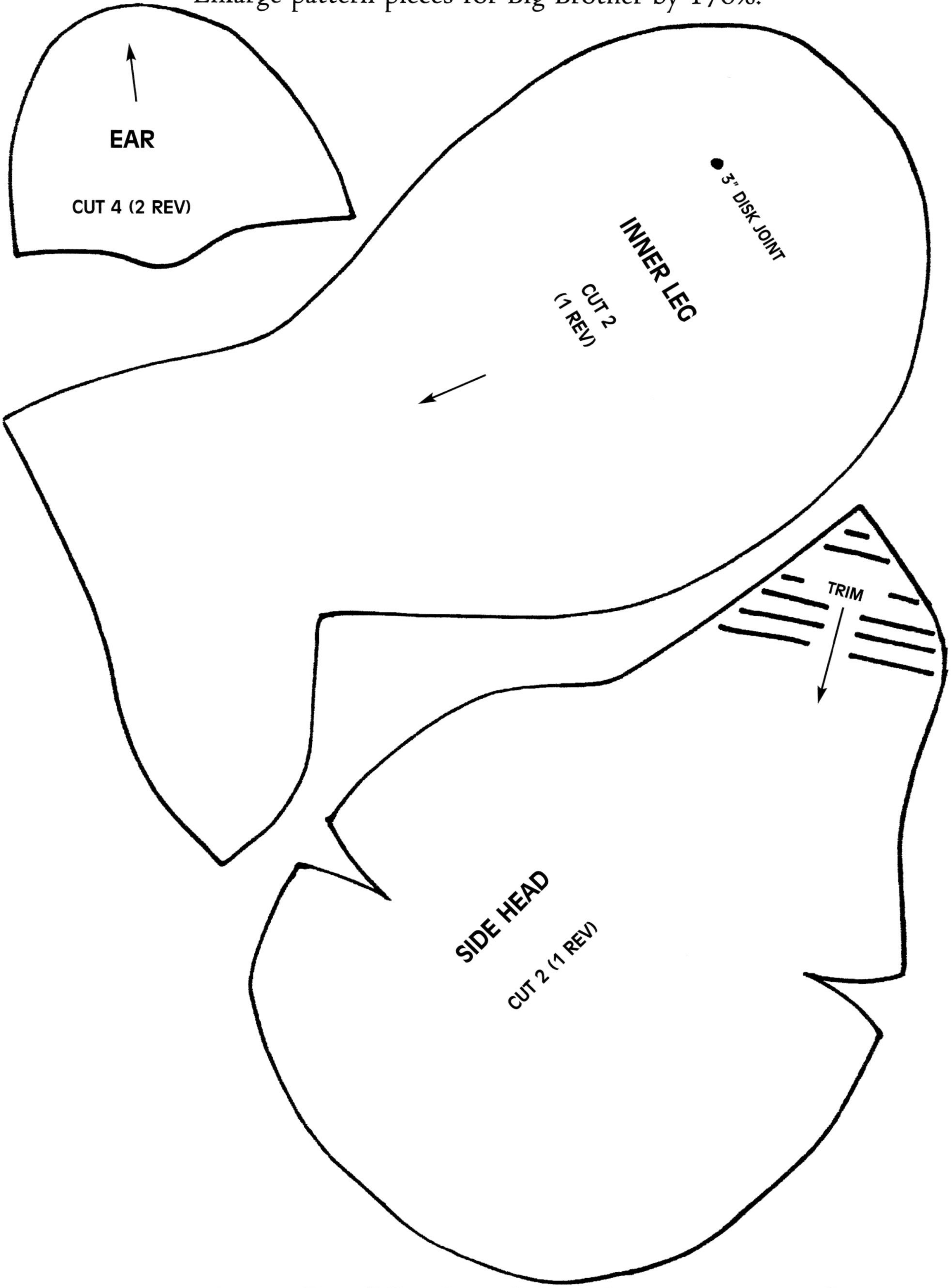

EAR
CUT 4 (2 REV)
3" DISK JOINT
INNER LEG
CUT 2
(1 REV)
TRIM
SIDE HEAD
CUT 2 (1 REV)

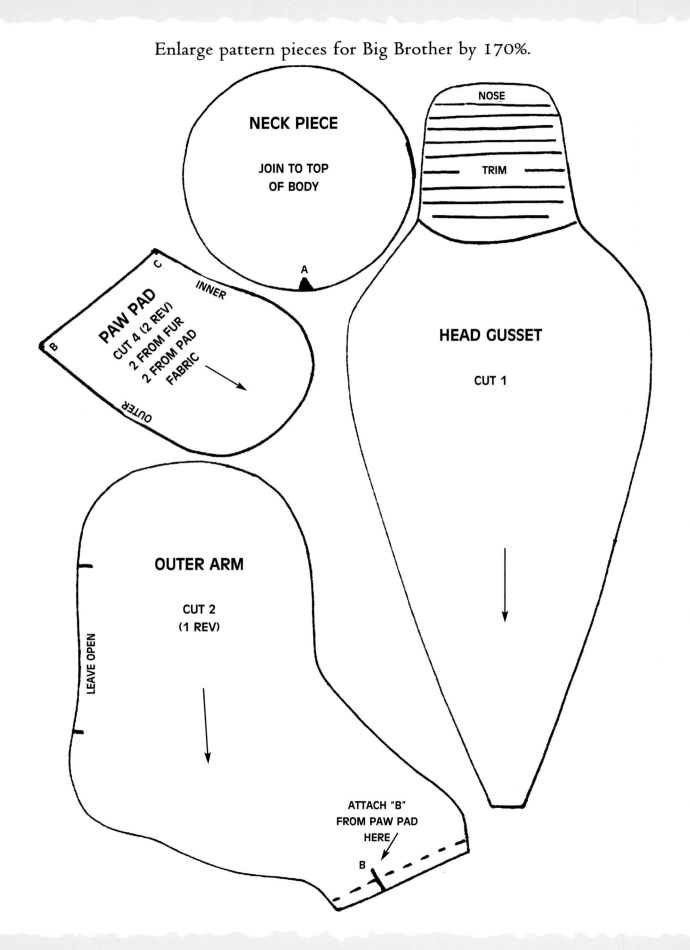

Enlarge pattern pieces for Big Brother by 170%.

NECK PIECE

JOIN TO TOP
OF BODY

A

NOSE

TRIM

HEAD GUSSET

CUT 1

C

INNER

PAW PAD

CUT 4 (2 REV)
2 FROM FUR
2 FROM PAD
FABRIC

B

OUTER

OUTER ARM

CUT 2
(1 REV)

LEAVE OPEN

ATTACH "B"
FROM PAW PAD
HERE

B

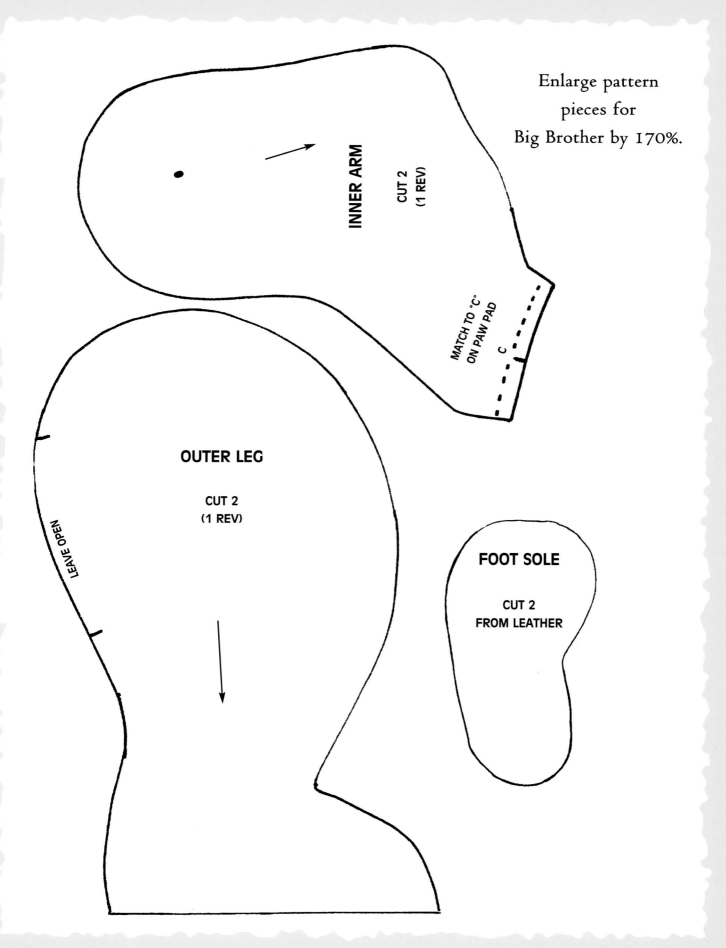

Enlarge pattern
pieces for
Big Brother by 170%.

INNER ARM

CUT 2
(1 REV)

MATCH TO "C"
ON PAW PAD

C

OUTER LEG

CUT 2
(1 REV)

LEAVE OPEN

FOOT SOLE

CUT 2
FROM LEATHER

Enlarge pattern pieces for Big Brother by 170%.

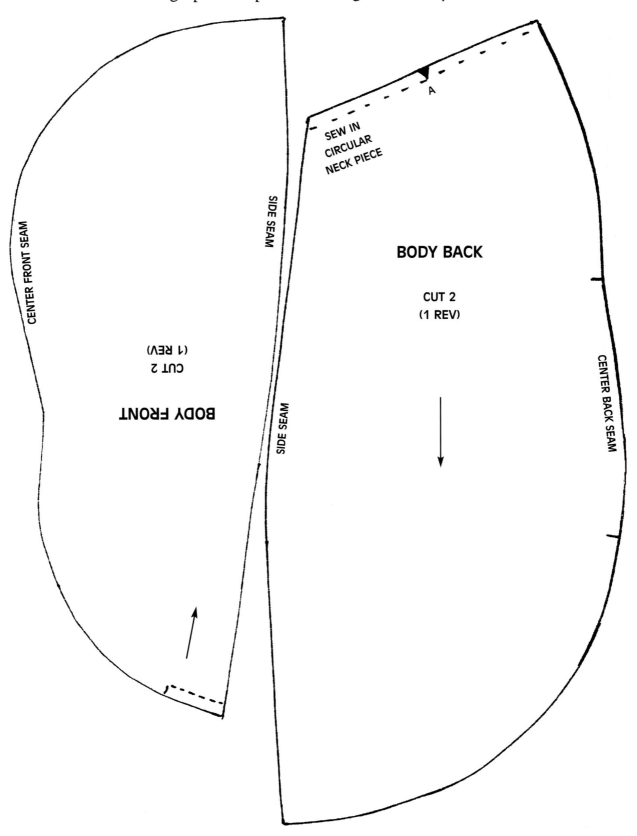

United States of America
Intercal Trading Group
For Helmbold and Norton mohair
Tel: (949) 645-9396
Fax: (949) 645-5471
www.intercaltg.com

Edinburgh Imports, Inc
For Schulte mohair
Tel: (805) 376-1700
Fax: (805) 376-1711
www.edinburgh.com

South Africa
Teddytech
For Schulte mohair
Tel: +27-31-312-7755
Fax: +27-31-312-9564
E-mail: ebeaton@global.co.za

Honeydew Bears
For Helmbold mohair
Tel/fax: +27 11 678 5834
E-mail: honeydewbears@wol.co.za

Great Britain
Oakley Fabrics
For Schulte mohair
Tel: 01582-424-828
Fax: 01582-455-274
www.oakleyfabrics.co.uk

Australia
Gerry's Teddy & Craft Designs
For Schulte mohair
Tel: +61 (07) 3846-5959
Fax +61 (07) 3846-5960
www.gerrys.com.au

Beary Cheap Bear Supplies
For Helmbold mohair
Tel: 07-55203455
Fax: 07-55203411
www.bearycheap.com

About the Authors

Janet Viveiros

Collecting and being surrounded with interesting pleasures began in the early 1980's with a career as an import agent in gifts and housewares. The business expanded into one that represented the best of African handcrafted giftware covering all things creative and beautiful — even today an all-consuming passion for Janet.

It was in 1992 whilst in Europe that the concept of South Africa's first retail store catering to the serious arctophile was born. After extensive research, *The Bear Collection* was opened in Johannesburg in March 1993 indulging new and would-be teddy collectors with all the leading imports (Steiff, Hermann, Dean's, Merrythought, North American Bear Company) and many more.

Now in its tenth year, Janet and her staff have created a huge awareness of the Teddy Bear industry. They offer regular classes and supply the best, imported mohair and allied accessories for bear makers. In addition to creating new bears, they restore treasured oldies — an art form that comes from the soul!

Janet's love of the teddy bear probably started as a young girl of 4 when she left her birthplace in England along with her teddy to settle on the far off shores of Australia. That teddy bear traveled the world for some 20 years thereafter, always being the first on the list of packing items. To this day, Janet believes all travelers should have a teddy as a travel companion.

Michela Rae

Michela was born in South Africa and after many years in the big city, has now relocated to Plettenberg Bay, a small coastal town where she lives on a farm with her husband, Simon. Michela currently owns and runs an advertising business in Johannesburg, but her passion has always been with teddy bears. A lifetime obsession with the furry creatures started as a young child and has continued to this day. A keen collector and avid bear maker, Michela is also very interested in marketing South African bear artists to the rest of the world. This book is an opportunity to showcase their talent for everyone to see and enjoy. She is turning bear making into a full time career from her farm studio where she will run workshops and a showroom for bear makers and collectors.

"Making bears has been the most rewarding hobby I've ever experienced. I can't imagine anything more exciting than the creation of something you can actually hug rather than just look at. I can't recall ever having so much fun making something from scratch. The most incredible part of it for me is seeing my design on paper come to life in the fur, watching as each unique personality develops in my hands—what an experience. I hope that bear makers will enjoy this book as much as we have enjoyed putting it together."

A great big thank you from both of us to all the wonderful artists who contributed their patterns to this book, we couldn't have done it without you.